SH食OKU·IKU!

JAPANESE CONSCIOUS EATING FOR A LONG AND HEALTHY LIFE

BY MAKIKO SANO

Photography by Lisa Linder

Quadrille
PUBLISHING

Japanese Pickles, see page 90

CONSCIOUS EATING

Shoku-Iku is about a brand new relationship with food. It is conscious eating: ditching that just-grab-something attitude and believing that you deserve to be a little more mindful about the relationship between what you eat and your body. It is about choosing foods based on their power to invigorate, enliven, energise, fuel and give you true nutrition. When you do this you simply feel better, lighter and in control and — though initially you will have to put some thought into it — over time it will become a way of life.

My family instilled this mindful attitude to food in me as a child in Japan. Every morning my grandfather had a pint of water mixed with the juice of two squeezed lemons. I had to drink it with him (and I thought it was disgusting as a child!), but I still do the same to this day. We ate a selection of fish, vegetables, beans and miso soup at every meal. My grandfather played tennis until he was 97; my uncle lived to 100. Growing up, my memories are of my parents, aunts and uncles, grandparents and cousins, all of whom lived nearby, eating their evening meal together.

Sagen Ishizuka initiated the Shoku-Iku concept. This famous Japanese military doctor was also a pioneer of the macrobiotic diet. The philosophy is built on acquiring knowledge about what we eat, how we prepare it and how we put different foods together. The rules of Shoku-Iku are not strict or hard to follow, but truly common sense.

A Shoku-Iku way of eating is to create a few dishes — not just one alone — to place on the table and share. Even at breakfast, my mother will always have a wide selection of foods: an oil-free omelette, spinach or nori salad, miso soup and a piece of fruit. I love the idea of sharing food, as it makes each meal an occasion. It's great that even when I was a teenager, busy with friends and school, we still made time to sit as a family. And if you live alone, take the time to make a couple of quick and simple side dishes, to celebrate each meal time, honour your body and become more of a conscious eater.

This attention to the ritual of meal times will also help you to incorporate more variety in your diet, what we call the power of five. As you will read over the next few pages, this philosophy is to eat foods from five food groups that appeal to your five senses, that contain five tastes and which aim to reflect five colours.

The recipes in this book are mostly gluten free, but those that are not can easily be tweaked to suit a gluten-free diet. They are often, as is the Japanese way, rice based and rice is very easily digested. Many of the recipes swap meat for what we know in Japan as 'the meat of the garden', in other words vegetable protein sources such as beans and pulses. The recipes are largely dairy-free, as Japanese cuisine rarely features dairy produce.

All the recipes in this book use the healthiest cooking methods possible. Certainly there is no need to turn your oven on (or even to own an oven) and, in some cases, no cooking is required at all. The dishes are revitalising and tasty, but also simple, quick to prepare and budget friendly. Many of the dishes — and all the sauces — can be made in quantity and stored for later, to help cut down on food waste... Welcome to Shoku-Iku!

GO SHOKU-IKU!

Eat as wide a variety of foods as you can every day.

Choose locally grown and seasonal foods.

Establish a healthy rhythm to your daily meals, eating at regular times.

Choose to sit down, consciously enjoy and focus on your meals.

If you have a family, treat meal time as something sacred that you all do together.

Think about what you have eaten through the day and make the next meal choice something different, to balance your food groups.

Don't skip meals. It will lead to poor food choices later in the day.

Combine vegetables, fruits, milk, fish and beans in your daily diet. Avoid too much salt, sugar or fat.

The power of five

Colours
Tastes
Senses
Food groups
Cooking methods

The five colours

Learning to adopt the principles of the power of five into your daily diet is the key to unlocking a whole new way of eating. This Buddhist tradition arrived in Japan in the sixth century and is part of our way of life. By combining elements of all these colours in your meals whenever possible, you broaden the variety of foods you eat and ensure you are getting the healthiest mix of essential vitamins and minerals. My grandmother used to aim to eat 30 different foods a day. That is hard... but you should aim for 13–20 different foods every day. In other words, look at your eating habits and see if you focus on the same food types and colours — such as pasta — too heavily.

A food rainbow
We have become adept at checking sandwich packs for their calorie count, but we perhaps still don't think too carefully about the breadth of the food groups we choose from daily. In Japanese cooking we get automatic variety, because of the ever-present side dishes. A Japanese bento box, for instance, might include white rice with black sesame seeds, a red umeboshi (salt plum), a slice of sweet yellow omelette and green beans with black sesame sauce.

Look to see where you can incorporate this idea into your food choices. For example, if you pick up a sandwich at lunchtime, pick up a pot of edamame beans as well. Choose a sunshine-coloured fruit juice to accompany it. If you fancy a piece of lean steak, prepare a freshly chopped tomato salad on the side. You don't have to ditch the things you love. Just make sure you have a mix every day of your life.

Pick and mix
In our supermarket shop we tend to buy the same things week in week out, and this goes against the quest for variety. When you look at your shopping basket, it should reflect the five colours. Here are some ingredients you might want to start adding to your shop and using to create my Shoku-Iku dishes.

Green/blue

Broccoli
the intensely blue-green vegetable contains 150% of your daily vitamin C needs in a 100g serving.

Spinach
this deep garden-green vegetable is considered a superfood, as it is bursting with iron and potassium.

Edamame beans
a complete protein, with all nine essential amino acids. Also chock-full of vitamins B, C and K, even when frozen and defrosted.

Cucumber
the green skin is full of vitamin C, but this hydrating vegetable also contains silicon and sulphur, associated with reducing the risk of some cancers.

Red/orange

Carrot
the colour comes from high levels of antioxidant beta-carotene, which we convert into vitamin A.

Tomato
bursting with vitamins A, C and E and also rich in flavonoids, natural anti-inflammatories.

Sweet potato
another glorious orange- or purple-fleshed vegetable, rich with beta-carotene. A dash of fat, such as olive oil, helps the body release beta-carotene's benefits. My mum would wrap sweet potatoes in foil and bake them in the fire as an after-school snack. Delicious.

White

Cabbage
a great source of fibre. Use it fresh to make the most of its anti-inflammatory goodness and its rich potassium content.

Chinese leaves
these pale leaves are intensely hydrating, low in calories and aid sleep.

Mooli
not only is this root vegetable highly flavoursome, but it contains anti-carcinogenic phytochemicals and has decongestant properties.

Fish
a major source of omega-3 fatty acids, this can help to protect against a range of diseases, from cancer to heart disease, depression to arthritis.

White rice
a digestive aid and natural anti-inflammatory. Its protein is important for preserving lean body mass. Its manganese helps boost the immune system, while thiamine is important for cognitive processes.

Black/brown

Shiitake mushrooms
known for their immune system support, these are a good source of iron and antioxidants.

Buckwheat
this not only helps in keeping cholesterol levels low, but is also a good source of magnesium.

Seaweed
great for detoxing the system, this is rich in enzymes that aid digestion. It is also high in fibre.

Brown rice
rich in selenium, which reduces the risk of heart disease. It is also a slow energy release food, keeping you fuller for longer.

Black beans
the skins are an incredible source of phytonutrients. More fibre than chickpeas or lentils.

Black sesame seeds
rich in magnesium and calcium (found in the husk), the numerous health benefits of which include combatting disruptive sleep patterns. I crush the seeds in a mini-blender to ensure I keep all the goodness of the husk and store them in small jars.

Yellow

Soy beans
very rich in protein and manganese and a good source of iron, magnesium and copper. High in the phytoestrogens beneficial for menopausal women.

Pumpkin
plenty of fibre to keep you full up and a great source of unsaturated fat. The high beta-carotene content is essential for glowing skin.

Corn
a sunshine vegetable, rich in B vitamins and fibre.

The five tastes

Surprising palates is one way to get people to connect with what they are eating. Awakening all five tastes has been part of my culinary journey; it is when you trigger them that food really comes alive.

Cooking with fresh, healthy ingredients need never be a bland option. It is how you compose those tastes, what other flavours you balance them with, that makes meals exciting. Many of my recipes can use different sauces, depending on which taste you crave at that moment.

Sweet

Sweet tastes signal the presence of carbohydrates. In Japan, we eat only very small amounts of sweet things. One slice of cake would be shared between four people. It was appreciated more that way... you learned to truly savour sweet things. My great uncle still had all his teeth at 97! Many traditional Japanese sweets have alternatives to refined sugar at their base, for instance red bean paste or fruit, letting the fructose do the work. One of my favourite sweet ingredients is mirin, a sweet rice wine essential in Japanese cooking. You can make your own mirin by gently heating three parts of sake or vodka with one part of sugar.

Sour

Sour = acidity. Japanese rice vinegar delivers that sour hit, but is slightly less acidic and sweeter than its European counterpart. It is this vinegar added to sushi rice that adds that satisfying note, bringing the rice alive. The juice and zest of citrus fruits are of course the other familiar providers of sour taste sensations. The Japanese yuzu citrus is just being discovered here. This cross between a lemon, grapefruit and mandarin contains three times more vitamin C than a lemon, elevating it to a superfood in the sour realms.

Bitter

This is the most sensitive of all the tastes, not least because it helps us avoid foods that might not be good for us, or which may be under-ripe. However, it is a very complementary flavour when used sparingly, or with the right companions: think of how green olives flatter an aperitif. Some vegetables have a slightly bitter tone, such as aubergine, or spinach. Again, when cooked with complementary flavours, the bitterness adds a delicious roundness. My Lemon soy sauce dressing (see page 20) has delectable bitter notes.

Salt

As a chef, I am super-aware of the issues around salt. In Japan, the main source of salt in food is from soy sauce and miso. Unlike western chefs, though, and as you will see through the Shoku-Iku recipes, we tend to add very little salt during cooking. Nearly all the salt comes from the sauces or condiments used, so there is less 'hidden salt' than there can be in western food.

Soy sauce does contain the high levels of sodium found in table salt, but the fermentation process also produces peptides, which may limit the cardiovascular issues related to regular salt. Either way, try to look for traditionally made soy sauce; those from Japan usually are. You can also purchase low-sodium varieties. Recent studies on miso intake among Japanese adults have also shown that miso-containing diets tend to lower the risk of cardiovascular problems, despite its salt content. Since miso is seldom eaten alone, other cardio-supportive foods in miso soups and stir-fries might also play an important role.

Umami

The name of this subtle, pleasant savoury taste comes from the Japanese word 'umai', meaning delicious. It is a naturally occurring flavour found in the oils of certain vegetables, meat and fish. First recognised in Japan in 1908, the flavour was detected in asparagus, tomatoes, cheese and meat. However, another Japanese staple was where the umami flavour shone brightest. Dashi is a rich, tasty stock made from kombu (kelp) and often bonito flakes (for vegetarian or fish-based recipes, see page 18). It is widely used as a base in Japanese cooking. The essence of its savoury deliciousness is imparted by amino acids called glutamates. My Everyday soy sauce dressing (see page 19) has delicious umami flavours. You can also dial up the umami quotient of your food, if you eat dairy, by adding a little butter to a soy sauce-based dish, or sprinkling a bit of Parmesan cheese into a miso sauce.

The five senses

How often have you sat down to eat without consciously thinking about the effects your food is having on you? Perhaps most of the time? All of the time? The underlying principle of Shoku-Iku asks us to be mindful and fully awake to all five senses: taste, smell, sight, sound and touch. Too often we are in too much of a hurry. Taking time to eat slowly, so you can be more aware of your senses, is really important.

In Japan, fulfilling all the senses is second nature. It reconnects us to what we are eating.

Sound

I love to experience the sounds of different restaurants depending on the food they are creating. From the quiet stillness of a high-end ryotei restaurant, where due respect is shown for the exquisitely prepared sushi dishes, to the happy, boisterous noise of an izakaya (Japanese tapas bar). It's as if the food invokes a certain atmosphere. At home, if you are bringing a selection of dishes to the table for a sharing meal, it always creates a jovial, bonding, informal and light-hearted atmosphere. But listening to the sounds of food is also key to our enjoyment. The crisp crunch of fresh vegetables is, in itself, invigorating and some researchers think sound can influence and enhance flavour. Top chef Heston Blumenthal famously gives his diners headphones to enhance specific dishes with their own soundtrack!

Sight

Seeing a plate of vibrant colours is uplifting and appetising. In Japan, even a lunchtime bento box is filled with colour: yellow omelette, bright green edamame, pink salmon, white rice and black sesame seeds. Once you get used to seeing these kinds of colours, other foods can appear bland. You can easily dial up the vibrancy of whatever you are cooking simply by the addition of bright pickles, a scattering of shredded nori or some sliced cherry tomatoes. Even consider your tableware. In Japan, food presentation has been raised to an art form, but just having a selection of beautiful dishes, bowls and utensils elevates what you have prepared and makes it that bit more enticing.

Touch

Touch is vital to me as a chef, whether it's learning how to handle food, or eating and appreciating its various textures. Even the very act of chopping herbs, sprinkling seeds or rolling sushi connects me to what I am preparing and therefore to what I am about to eat. It also helps you to eat a good variety of foods; you wouldn't want everything to 'feel' the same.

Carry that same sense into your tableware. Japanese meals often require you to pick up vessels of miso, dishes of pickles, or eat with chopsticks. Connecting with the smooth wood of a bamboo chopstick, the delicate touch of a porcelain dish or the rougher texture of a stoneware bowl adds to the overall sensation experience.

Smell

Through my recipes you will learn to prepare food with some of the more underused cooking processes. Steaming is a method I love not least because, as you steam food, a host of delicious scents rise into the air. The sense of smell starts the longing to taste the food. Eighty per cent of what we perceive to be the flavour of food is actually down to its aroma. Smell also opens up our memory pathways. There's something very comforting about preparing a food whose scent takes you back to a place in your childhood or a happy event.

Taste

Ultimately, taste elevates food from a simple question of nourishment to a pleasurable experience. As you become more familiar with Japanese dishes, you will see that many of the taste twists come from extra condiments, sauces and sprinkles: the umami flavour of a splash of dashi; the deep saltiness of soy sauce; the heat of a little sake or wasabi. Minced nori, shiso leaves and citrussy yuzu zest shavings are other things you may learn to experiment with, to excite the taste buds and give your food an authentic Japanese feel, along with mirin, vinegar and ginger.

Japanese Garden, see page 60

The five food groups

In East Asian tradition, the number five has always been important. The traditional Japanese calendar has a five day weekly cycle, while much of the Japanese aesthetic is built around the five elements of water, fire, earth, metal and air: the flame under a nabemono cooking pot; the sound of a water feature in a courtyard.

The foundation of Shoku-Iku eating is based around this principle of five, in this case five food groups, which you should select from every day. When I'm eating out in Japan I am always struck by how groups of diners, even without thinking, balance out their food choices. It's as if they subconsciously know what is missing and will order an extra dish to balance out what they have already selected.

Grains
(aim for 5–6 servings a day)

Grains (including rice and noodles) are an important source of nutrients and dietary fibre. They are high in several B vitamins (thiamin, riboflavin, niacin and folate) and minerals (iron, magnesium and selenium). These play key roles in both our metabolism and boosting our nervous and immune systems. They also help the body release energy from protein, fats and carbohydrates. Their fibre content may help to lower cholesterol and maintain a healthy heart. Because of their iron content they also help maintain iron levels in the blood, which is especially beneficial for women. To make the most of their nutrients, combine them with vitamin C-rich foods and eat them with proteins and carbohydrates.

Tip: When preparing white rice, always rinse it first under cold running water until the water runs clear (see page 110 for how to cook Japanese rice).

The five elements

As with a macrobiotic diet, Shoku-Iku is all about balance through variety, making sure you acknowledge all five elements (wood, fire, earth, water, metal) in your daily meals.

Once you get used to balancing from the food groups you can adjust them according to your mood. To feel more grounded, make sure you take in enough earth foods; to help increase your stamina, up the fire foods. If you are feeling a little withdrawn, cut down on metal foods.

WOOD	FIRE	EARTH	METAL	WATER
Leafy green vegetables, raw, steamed or simmered, vinegars and lemon.	Garlic, ginger, spring onions, mild spices, nuts and seeds.	Sweet root and ground vegetables cooked into a soup or stew.	Pressure-cooked or long-cooked grains such as brown rice, daikon and pickles.	Miso soups, bean soups, miso.

Vegetables
(aim for 5–6 servings a day)

When trying to balance your diet, keeping a food diary for a week can be a real eye opener. As with the usual nutritional advice, ensuring you eat adequate quantities of vegetables every day is vital. If you are choosing too many comfort foods, then starting to adjust this to fulfil your daily quota is made easier by preparing dishes already laden with vegetables.

High in dietary fibre and antioxidants, vegetables should be the cornerstone to every meal. If you're not cooking a vegetarian or vegetable-filled dish then add a side dish of green salad leaves or grated carrot, or nibble on an appetiser of radishes, red pepper sticks or edamame. These strategies can easily up your vegetable intake with virtually no effort. My Japanese garden (see page 60) is made with pumpkin, turnip, mooli, broccoli and sugar snap peas, so there are five vegetables in one dish.

Fish and meat, eggs and beans, nuts and seeds
(aim for 3–5 servings a day)

Protein is a vital source of nutrients, for healthy bones, muscles, skin and blood. With fats and carbohydrates, proteins also provide the calories we need.

In Japan, the majority of our protein comes from fish. Not only is fish high in omega-3 fatty acids, but it is inherently lean. When choosing meat, always select lean cuts of pork, chicken or beef.

Tip: we often sprinkle fish with sake before cooking, to refresh the surface and remove 'fishy' odours.

The alternative to fish and meat, highly popular in Japan, are soy beans. We refer to these as 'the meat of the garden' and they have all the benefits of protein but with none of the downsides.

Eggs are another great and easy source of protein and feature in Japanese cooking often, especially at breakfast time when omelette is a favourite.

Not just an afterthought, nuts and seeds should also be part of your daily food. These little extras are packed with nutrients including B vitamins, vitamin E, iron, zinc and magnesium.

Tip: For a lighter option to a bowl of nuts, munch on some salted edamame beans (also packed with protein).

Fruits
(aim for 2–3 servings a day)

Other than the obvious vitamin and fibre benefits of fruit, one of the bonuses to a chef is that it contains natural sugars (fructose). Refined sugars are known dietary baddies and I try to steer clear. In many of my pudding recipes I use fruit to add sweetness, especially when the fruit has been poached or steamed, reducing its juices to a sweet sticky sauce.

The five food groups of Shoku-Iku encourage the cutting down to a bare minimum of sugary sweets. If you can limit your sweet intake and start to think of fruit as your sweet treat, you will improve your overall diet. A few slices of nashi (Japanese pear), melon, or ume (Japanese plum), made into balls and wrapped in rice make a delicious treat. And check out my Fruit buns recipe (see page 65).

Dairy
(no more than 2 servings a day)

In modern-day Japan, all manner of cheeses and dairy products can be found on the streets, thanks to the pizza and coffee companies that are springing up. However, dairy was not historically part of the diet and is still little used in home cooking. Japanese hot drinks of green tea or miso don't require the addition of milk. A Japanese breakfast seldom includes cereal and milk, although my mother does like to eat yogurt at breakfast time. There are certain indulgent treats we do love — green tea ice cream is a particular favourite — but for the most part, milk is not a common ingredient in a Japanese kitchen.

The five cooking methods

The cooking method is vital to the appearance, flavour and texture of a dish. Japanese cooks hardly ever roast food, but that's not to say we don't employ plenty of other methods. Take kaiseki cuisine, for instance, the Japanese chef's art of using various cooking styles to add up to a complete experience. Kaiseki meals usually start with the most delicate flavours and textures, such as a few slices of sashimi. This is followed by soup or simmered vegetables in broth. Next is grilled fish or meat. The meal then winds down with rice, soup and pickles. Dessert is always light; perhaps a perfect slice of melon, or a refreshing dish of green tea ice cream. While none of us would produce that on a daily basis, it is easy to make three or four simple dishes, for example grilled fish, miso soup and steamed or raw vegetables, that echo the principle.

All the techniques I favour are gentle on the food — retaining the nutrients — and also quick.

Steam and microwave

Many of my recipes are cooked by steaming which is a beautifully simple, gentle and traditional way of cooking food. But as a busy mother, I also use the microwave as a super-speedy way of producing the same results. Heavenly steamed sea bream (see page 47) can be made in the microwave and is ready to eat in four minutes.

- **Steaming has a myriad of benefits. It not only retains food's nutrients, but also its moisture and freshness.**

- **Both steaming and microwaving help retain the vibrant colours and natural flavours of your food.**

- **Steaming softens food fibres, making them easily digestible.**

- **When you steam a meal there is no need for cooking oil or fat, so your food is lighter and healthier. And, because you can stack steamer dishes over a single heat source, it saves time, energy and money.**

Simmer

Simmering is an essential part of Japanese cooking. Nimono is a home-cooking style of simmering vegetables in seasoned broth. Shabu is its grander restaurant style, where a central bowl of simmered broth is used to 'wash' or lightly cook julienned vegetables and meats (see page 41). The key to simmering is low heat. This avoids the drab, soggy effects of high heat boiling. In Japan, the liquid from a simmered dish becomes part of the sauce.

- **Many of my recipes simmer and steam in shallow lidded pans with only a tiny amount of liquid.**

- **Simmering preserves the vibrant colours of the food.**

- **Liquids other than water can be used to add more flavour.**

Grill and fry

I love the scents that waft from food as you grill it. Many of the grilled Shoku-Iku recipes for fish, meat and vegetables have been marinated or 'rinsed' with flavouring ingredients, heightening that mouth-watering effect. The benefits of grilling over shallow frying or roasting are many.

- **Excess fats drip off and cook away, leaving less fat in the food.**

- **Vegetables retain more vitamins and minerals.**

- **The high heat seals in moisture and keeps food tender, so there's no need to add oil or butter.**

No-cook

Raw food is a way of life in Japan and not just in the well-known sushi and sashimi. The benefits of raw foods are tremendous.

- **Our bodies love the electrons that raw foods preserve and which are diminished in cooking: they literally burn up and break down.**

- **Cooking food destroys many of its natural enzymes. We need these enzymes to break down nutrients.**

- Essential vitamins and minerals are lost through the cooking process. Many nutritionists believe we should be eating one raw dish or accompaniment at every meal, for example fruit with breakfast, salad with lunch and sashimi at dinner.

- Raw fruit and veg tend to be more bulky with fibre, so help keep us feeling fuller for longer. They also have a high natural water content, so they hydrate as well as nourish.

- Chewing raw food is an excellent workout for your gums and jaw. The Japanese are crazy about chewing. We really see it as essential exercise and will deliberately select foods that require more chewing.

Sushi

This is the food most associated with Japanese cuisine across the world. In its traditional form, sushi delivers all the goodness of raw fish, which has always been Shoku-Iku and, these days, that researchers increasingly believe is one of the keys to a long and healthy life. I have also included some new ways with sushi in this book, including lightly cooked vegetables, for vegetarian and vegan diets.

- Ideal for entertaining, Shoku-Iku sushi dishes are stunning looking, appealing to the sense of sight, as well as taste.

- Rice is light on the digestion, so a sushi meal is easy for your body to process.

Julienning vegetables

The julienne cut ensures each slice cooks evenly and thoroughly by increasing the surface area exposed to heat.

Remove the ends of the vegetable and trim the outer edges to make four straight sides.
This makes it easier to produce a uniform cut. (Use the trimmings for stocks.)
Neatly slice into squares, then into sticks roughly 5cm long and 3mm squared.

If you are nervous about hand-cutting julienne, invest in a mandolin for speed and ease.

Foundation dishes

All-rounder sauces and stocks

These are the foundations to all Shoku-Iku dishes. Once you have learnt how to create these, you can mix and match, using them to add the flavours you fancy to most Shoku-Iku recipes.

Stocks

Basic dashi (stock)

Dashi is a fundamental building block of Japanese food. It is a stock, usually made from bonito flakes, dried kelp and, sometimes, dried sardines or anchovies. There are no animal fats in it at all.

My grandmother would mix them herself to make her meals. My basic stock these days is made from packaged dried kelp and bonito flakes. Feel free to scale the recipe down if you don't think you'll need this much. You can use it straight away, or cover and keep it in the fridge for five to seven days (or up to one month in the freezer).

Makes 2 litres
— 10 x 5cm pieces of dried kelp
— 50g bonito flakes

Pour two litres of water into a saucepan. Add the kelp and set aside for at least one hour and up to three or four if you have time. The deeply savoury, umami flavour of the kelp will seep into the water.

Set the saucepan over a medium heat and bring it to the boil. Reduce the heat to its lowest when the kelp starts 'dancing' (as my grandmother used to say). Cook at the gentlest simmer for 20–30 minutes. Turn off the heat and add ½ cup of water to cool it down.

Add the bonito flakes and leave for about one minute. Strain the stock through a sieve into a bowl, pressing down on the bonito flakes with a spoon to extract the maximum flavour.

Vegetarian dashi

Makes about 1 litre
— 5 x 1.5cm pieces of dried kelp
— 5 dried shiitake mushrooms

Pour one litre of cold water into a glass bowl or pot. Add the kelp and shiitake mushrooms. Cover and refrigerate for at least six hours (I usually leave it overnight). Strain through a sieve into a bowl, pressing down with a spoon for the maximum flavour.

Motoko's (my mother's) dashi

A dashi made with this as its liquid base has more flavour than the others and is more nutritious, due to the goodness of brown rice. It is meant to form the liquid part of the two dashis to the left.

— 50g brown rice

Rinse the rice and tip it into a medium saucepan. Set over a medium heat and cook, stirring, until the husks start to split. You will know when this happens, you can see it (but you may need a bit of practice to spot it), so go by your nose: you will smell the brown rice aroma when the husk splits to release its flavour.

Pour in one litre of water and cook on medium-low heat (enough so the rice is 'dancing') for 30 minutes.

Pass through a sieve into a bowl and top up with liquid to form the base of a Basic or Vegetarian dashi.

Noodle soup stock

This is easy, made from very basic Japanese ingredients and, of course, my dashi stock.

Makes about 1.2 litres
— 800ml Basic or Vegetarian dashi (see left)
— 200ml mirin
— 200ml soy sauce

Add everything to a saucepan and bring to a simmer.

Soup stock

This one is, if anything, even easier, as you don't even need a pre-prepared dashi stock.

Makes about 1.2 litres
— 200ml mirin
— 200ml soy sauce
— 10g bonito flakes
— 1 x 5cm piece of dried kelp

Pour the mirin into a saucepan and bring to the boil. Add the soy sauce, pour in 800ml of water and return to the boil. Add the bonito flakes and kelp and turn off the heat.

Let it cool. Keep in the fridge and use within 10 days.

Dressings

In Japanese food, we use a lot of dressings, together with small amounts of sauce, to add flavour to our dishes. This is because traditional Japanese food is quite plain, especially in a Shoku-Iku style of eating, without many strong tastes. So it's nice to add additional flavours into the food. Many contain soy sauce and we enjoy its umami flavour.

These dressings are not thick, they are light and tasty, not high in calories or oily, and you can use them for anything you like: salad, chicken or fish, or even with sushi. So, next time you reach for the mayonnaise, remember these lighter recipes and give them a try instead.

Everyday soy sauce dressing

The name says it all: there's almost no Japanese dish that this won't complement.

Makes enough for 4
— 2 tbsp mirin
— 2 tbsp soy sauce, ideally light soy sauce
— 2 tbsp rice vinegar

Pour all the ingredients into a saucepan and heat to a simmer, then allow the pan to cool completely. Covered and kept in the fridge, the dressing will last for seven days.

Sweet soy dressing

This is nice with meat, prawns or salads.

Makes enough for 4
— 2 tsp runny honey
— 4 tsp whole grain mustard
— 4 tsp lemon juice
— 3 tbsp grapeseed oil
— pinch of salt

Mix all the ingredients together well.

Sesame salad sprinkle dressing

If you eat whole sesame seeds, they go straight through you. But, if you blend them to a powder, you get all their nutrition. Whenever one of my recipes calls for 'crushed' sesame seeds, it means seeds whizzed to a powder in a blender.

This is especially good with quite plain, steamed dishes, or over salads.

Makes enough for 4
— 1 tbsp soy sauce
— 2 tbsp caster sugar
— 3 tbsp rice vinegar
— 1 tbsp white miso
— 2 tbsp white sesame seeds, crushed
  (see recipe introduction)

Pour the soy sauce and sugar into a saucepan and simmer until the sugar has dissolved.

Add the vinegar, miso and crushed sesame. Covered and kept in the fridge, it will last for seven days.

Rosemary soy sauce dressing

This dressing is wonderful with meat, in fact it's a bit of a westernised flavour. But it's also great with Shabu shabu (see page 41).

Makes 300ml
— 15cm sprig of rosemary
— 2 bay leaves
— 300ml soy sauce
— 2 garlic cloves

Sterilise a jar: I usually fill it with boiling water, leave it for three or four minutes, then tip it upside down to remove the water and leave it on a clean cloth to dry out completely.

Place everything in the sterilised jar. Leave it in a cool, dark place for a minimum of two weeks and up to four months. It's now ready to use; there's no need to strain out the bits.

Perfect with beer dressing

This is my dad's recipe; every time he has a beer he has this dressing on his food! It's great for most summer dishes: salads, or anything you eat with salads, or even with sashimi.

Makes about 300ml
— 1 apple
— ½ pear
— 1 onion
— 1 garlic clove
— 200ml soy sauce
— 60ml sake or vodka
— 3 tbsp brown sugar
— 2 tbsp white miso
— 2 tbsp sesame oil
— 2 tbsp white sesame seeds, crushed
  (see page 19)
— 2 tbsp whole white sesame seeds
— 1 tbsp chilli powder

Blend the apple, pear, onion and garlic in a blender or food processor. Add the soy sauce and the sake and blend again.

Transfer to a saucepan, add the sugar and miso and set over a low heat until the sauce thickens slightly.

Turn off the heat and add the sesame oil, crushed sesame, whole sesame seeds and chilli.

Let it cool and put it in a sterilised jar (see page 19) to keep in the fridge. It will keep for up to four weeks.

Lemon soy sauce dressing

My uncle found that vodka makes a good alternative to sake. Mirin is made from sake and sugar and, in the many places where sake is not available, vodka is a successful choice. My uncle, by the way, came across this substitution after many experimentations. Whisky, apparently, was an abject failure...

Makes about 400ml / Serves about 5
— 140ml sake or vodka
— 60g caster sugar
— 100ml lemon juice
— 200ml soy sauce
— 50g bonito flakes
— 1 x 10cm piece of dried kelp

Pour the sake and sugar into a saucepan and bring to the boil, then turn the heat off. Add all the other ingredients and set aside for four to six hours.

Strain the dressing into a bowl, pressing down on the bonito flakes to extract the maximum flavour. Covered, it will keep in the fridge for one month.

Shabu shabu dressing

This is a lighter dressing version of the heartier sauce (see page 41).

Makes enough for 2
— 2 tbsp whole white sesame seeds
— 2 tbsp white sesame seeds, crushed
  (see page 19)
— 2 tbsp rice vinegar
— 3 tbsp soy sauce
— 4 tbsp hemp or grapeseed oil
— ½ onion, grated
— 1 thumb of root ginger, grated
— 1 garlic clove, crushed or grated
— 1 tsp sea salt

Put the whole sesame seeds, crushed sesame, vinegar and soy sauce in a jar and mix well.

Add the oil and mix gently along with the onion, ginger, garlic and salt.

Garden soy sauce dressing

This is very light and full of nutrition with a lot of vegetables inside it. It's nice with salad or — surprisingly — with beef.

Makes about 300ml / Serves about 6
— 1 apple, grated
— 1 carrot, grated
— 1 onion, grated
— 100ml soy sauce
— 100ml rice vinegar
— 80g honey or brown sugar

Simply mix all the ingredients together and it's ready to serve.

How to form sushi

In the Sushi chapter (see pages 100–121), you will need a little knowledge about how to form sushi rolls and nigiri. Neither of these are at all difficult, but these step-by-step guides will help you along.

Nigiri

Rub grapeseed oil or mayonnaise into your palms and fingers. Take 20g of prepared sushi rice (see pages 104 and 110) in your right hand, if you are right-handed. (Or reverse all the instructions if you are left-handed.) Hold the prawn (or other topping) in your left hand, across the base of your fingers.

Place the rice on top of the fish. Put your right index finger on top of the rice. Wrap your left hand around your right index finger, squeezing gently to make a nice shape. Turn your nigiri so the fish is on top, still placed over the base of the fingers.

Repeat the wrapping and squeezing steps to form a neat, compact piece of nigiri. Do not squash the rice together too hard; all movements should be gentle.

Now smooth the edges of the prawn or other topping into an organic, graceful curve, with no corners: the topping should drape elegantly over the rice.

Sushi rolls

Place a half sheet of nori near the bottom of a sushi rolling mat, rough side up and shiny side down. Place 150g of prepared sushi rice (see pages 104 and 110) in the middle. Spread it out gently with your fingers to form an even covering all over the seaweed, leaving a 1cm strip empty at the top edge. Place the filling in a straight line across the middle of the rice.

Gently slide both thumbs under the mat and rest your middle fingers on the filling. Lift the edge of the mat and seaweed nearest to you over the filling. Lift up the leading edge of the mat with your right hand, if you are right-handed. (Or simply reverse all the instructions if you are left-handed.) Roll, with your left hand supporting the roll. Pull gently on the mat with your right hand.

Gently squeeze the mat to form a tight roll. Remove the mat. With a very sharp knife, cut the roll in half. Put the halves together and cut into six pieces in total, wiping the blade between each cut.

Inside-out sushi rolls

Many of my Shoku-Iku sushi recipes have the rice on the outside and the seaweed in the centre. To make these rolls, follow the instructions above but, after spreading out the rice, carefully flip over the whole piece, rice and seaweed, before adding the fillings.

Simmering is a very precise way of cooking, as heated water covers and surrounds food, maintaining a relatively constant temperature. This means the food cooks really evenly. It's a great choice for liquid-based dishes that contain a variety of ingredients, such as soups, stocks and noodles.

One of the most frequent questions that I get asked as a chef is: how can you tell when water is simmering, rather than boiling? The technical answer is that the liquid is somewhere between 82–96°C (180–205°F). For those without a thermometer, don't worry! The clues are also easy to see. A liquid for poaching should be flat and inactive, but a good simmering pan is slightly hotter. As a pan comes to a simmer you will be able to see small bubbles forming at the bottom and slowly rising to the top, but not aggressively or rapidly as you would see in a rolling boil.

This slow but gentle cooking technique helps to tenderise tougher cuts of meat. It is a gentler way to cook than boiling, so helps keep the food from breaking up, while the gradual nature of the process allows time for flavours to infuse and develop. More often than not, in my recipes, the simmering liquid will later form part of the dish. And as is the Shoku-Iku way, the cooking flavours are herb- and spice-based, so there's no need to load the simmering pan with salt prior to cooking.

JAPANESE CELLOPHANE NOODLE
(or vermicelli) **SOUP**

Cellophane noodles are made from potato and bean starch. This is very simple to make and filling, but easy for your body to digest. If you would like a vegetarian version, simply replace the mackerel with shiitake mushrooms. Smoked mackerel has quite a strong flavour, so I use it here as part of the 'stock'.

Serves 2–3

— **5 Iceberg lettuce leaves**
— **1 small smoked mackerel fillet**
— **1 medium onion, finely sliced**
— **½ thumb of root ginger, finely sliced**
— **50g Japanese cellophane noodles, or vermicelli**
— **pinch of sea salt and freshly ground black pepper**
— **1 spring onion, finely sliced**

Cut the lettuce and mackerel into bite-sized pieces. Soak the onion slices in water for 15 minutes.

Bring 500ml of water to the boil in a saucepan, add the lettuce, onion and ginger and simmer for three to four minutes until the onion softens. Add the fish and noodles and simmer over a medium heat for two or three minutes, until the noodles soften.

As you have the smoked mackerel flavour in the soup you won't need much salt (if any), but taste and see; I like to add a pinch of ground black pepper.

Ladle into a bowl and sprinkle with the spring onion.

RICE NOODLES WITH MUSHROOM BROTH

This is very filling and has all the vegetables within it. Again there's a very authentically Asian feel to this broth.

Serves 2

— **1 tsp kelp flakes**
— **40g rice noodles**
— **4 shiitake mushrooms, finely sliced**
— **½ thumb of root ginger, grated**
— **1 tsp light soy sauce**
— **½ tsp sea salt**
— **½ tsp freshly ground black pepper**
— **½ tsp sesame oil**
— **1 tsp white sesame seeds**
— **1 spring onion, sliced into julienne**
— **a little finely chopped chilli** (optional)

Pour 600ml of water into a saucepan and bring to the boil.

Add the kelp flakes and rice noodles and simmer for three minutes, until the noodles soften.

Add the mushrooms, ginger, soy sauce, salt and pepper, then turn the heat off and add the sesame oil, sesame seeds and spring onion.

Serve in bowls, adding chilli if you want a little spice.

DANCING PRAWNS

This is really rich in umami flavours and is very easy to make. The flavour of the prawns mixes beautifully with those of the sesame oil and leek.

Serves 2–3

— ½ leek, sliced into julienne
— 5 oyster mushrooms, sliced 1cm thick
— 250g large head-on prawns
— 5 tbsp sake
— 1 tsp sea salt
— 3–4 drops sesame oil
— 1 tsp soy sauce
— 1 spring onion, sliced into julienne

Place the leek in a saucepan that has a lid. Lay the mushrooms on the bed of leek and the prawns on top of those

Add the sake, cover and cook over a high heat until the sake starts to steam and the prawns start to 'dance' (as my grandmother used to say) in the liquid, then reduce the heat to medium so the pot is just simmering and add the salt, sesame oil and soy sauce. Cover again and continue to simmer for two or three minutes.

Transfer to a serving plate and sprinkle with the spring onion.

EDAMAME SOUP

When you add soy milk to a soup, it makes it thicker
and more creamy.

Serves 2

— 1 tbsp rapeseed oil
— ½ onion, finely chopped
— 200g potato, finely chopped
— 300g frozen edamame beans, defrosted
— 100ml soy milk
— pinch of sea salt and freshly ground
   black pepper
— 3 mint leaves, finely chopped

Pour the oil into a saucepan set over a medium heat,
add the onion and potato and cook until the onion
softens. Add the edamame and 450ml of water and
simmer until the potato is tender.

Blend it into a smooth soup, then return it to the
saucepan and add the soy milk. Return to a simmer
and cook for three minutes. DO NOT boil it, or the
soy milk could curdle.

Season, add the mint and serve, warm or cold.

SPICY EDAMAME

Serve this as a side dish. It is a way to make the
nutritional goodness of edamame a bit more sexy!

Serves 2

For the sauce
— 2 tbsp light soy sauce
— 1 garlic clove, grated
— ½ thumb of root ginger, grated
— 1 red or green chilli, finely chopped
— 2 tsp mixed sesame seeds
— 1½ tbsp sesame oil

For the edamame
— 1 tsp sea salt
— 250g frozen edamame beans, defrosted

Mix all the ingredients for the sauce in a bowl.

Pour two litres of water into a saucepan and bring
to the boil. Add the sea salt and edamame. Simmer
for three minutes, then drain in a sieve.

Add the warm edamame to the sauce and mix
with a spoon or your hands.

Serve immediately, as this is nicest when it's warm.

SOBA SOUP

This is a main dish. It is usually served in a tureen on the table for people to help themselves into their own small bowls, returning for seconds if they want. Soba noodles are made from buckwheat but many also have wheat flour added, so check the packet if you are avoiding wheat.

Serves 2

— **250g soba noodles**
— **5 tbsp Noodle soup stock** (see page 18),
  plus more if needed
— **1 leek, finely sliced**
— **100g pork belly, cut into 5mm-thick slices**
— **½ fillet of sea bass, cut into 2cm slices**
— **½ x 350g block of tofu, cut into 1cm pieces**
— **handful of kale, cut into 1cm pieces**

Bring two litres of water to the boil in a large saucepan. Add the noodles and cook for four to five minutes. Strain them through a sieve, reserving the cooking liquid. Rinse the noodles under cold water.

Measure 1 litre of the noodle cooking liquid and return it to the rinsed-out saucepan set over a medium heat. Add the Noodle soup stock and return the noodles. Add the leek, pork, sea bass, tofu and kale, cover and bring to the simmer.

Simmer for two to three minutes. Taste and see if you would like to add more soup stock, then adjust the seasonings accordingly and serve.

PAN TAI

In Japanese, 'tai' is the word for sea bream. So the name of this dish just means sea bream cooked in a pan!

Serves 2

— **240g brown rice**
— **1 whole sea bream or sea bass,
  scaled and cleaned**
— **5g root ginger, finely sliced**
— **300ml Motoko dashi** (see page 18)
— **1 chilli, finely chopped**
— **1 quantity Everyday soy sauce dressing
  or Lemon soy sauce dressing**
  (see pages 19 and 20)

Soak the brown rice in warm water for 30 minutes, then drain. Preheat the grill on its highest setting.

Lay the fish on a tray, dry it inside and out with kitchen paper, then grill it on both sides until its skin is a little brown.

Put the ginger, rice and Motoko dashi in a large sauté pan and lay the fish on top. Cover and cook over a medium heat for six to seven minutes. Now reduce the heat to low and simmer for a further 15 minutes.

Increase the heat to high and cook for a final minute, then turn off the heat completely and leave, still covered, for 15 minutes.

Serve with the chilli sprinkled on top and your choice of soy sauce dressing.

CUCUMBER SOUP

This is best as a cold soup to serve in very warm weather, but you could also warm it up if you like. Use kelp instead of bonito for a vegetarian version.

Serves 2

— 1 cucumber, sliced into julienne
— ½ tsp grated garlic
— 1½ tbsp caster sugar
— ½ tsp sea salt
— ½ tbsp bonito or kelp flakes
— 1 spring onion, finely chopped
— 1 tbsp soy sauce
— sea salt
— 2 tbsp rice vinegar, or to taste
— 1 tsp white sesame seeds

Put the cucumber julienne in a bowl of ice-cold water and chill it in the fridge for 30 minutes.

Pour 400ml of water into a separate bowl and add the garlic, sugar, salt and bonito flakes. Bring to the simmer, then leave to cool completely. Add the spring onion and soy sauce, then season with salt and vinegar to taste.

Drain the cucumber and stir it into the soup, sprinkling the sesame seeds on top.

EGG AND TOFU DASHI SOUP

This could be a side dish or a main meal. It is elegant, with very subtle flavours.

Serves 2–3

For the soup base
— 400ml Basic dashi (see page 18)
— 1 tsp soy sauce
— ½ tsp sea salt
— 1 tsp sake

For the rest
— 350g packet of firm tofu, cut into 1cm pieces
— large handful of baby spinach
— 3 eggs, lightly beaten
— 2 spring onions, cut into 3cm slices on
   the diagonal

Add all the ingredients for the soup base to a saucepan and bring to the simmer. Add the tofu and return to the simmer. Add the spinach and pour in the beaten egg, slowly swirling it around with chopsticks. Increase the heat to medium and wait until the egg floats on top of the soup.

Serve in bowls sprinkled with the spring onions.

GINGER SARDINES

Image on page 38

This is a classic dish, one that my grandma's generation would make often, because sardines have always been (and still are) cheap and very good for you.

Serves 2

— **240g sardines** (4 fish), **gutted and rinsed**
— **50g mooli, cut into 1cm half moons**
— **1 tbsp honey**
— **1 tbsp mirin**
— **1 tbsp sake**
— **½ tbsp dashi flakes**
— **1cm cube of dried kelp**
— **½ thumb of root ginger, sliced into julienne**
— **1 tbsp soy sauce**
— **pinch of caster sugar**

Put the sardines into a sauté pan with all the other ingredients.

Pour in 200ml of water and seal the pan with foil. Set over a medium heat for 20 minutes, then serve.

VEGETABLE BROTH

Image on page 39

This is full of goodness, perfect for winter as it's so filling. If I have this at lunchtime, I can't eat dinner!

Serves 2–3

— **30g dried shiitake mushrooms**
— **50g carrots, finely chopped**
— **50g onion, finely chopped**
— **50g leeks, finely chopped**
— **50g cabbage, finely chopped**
— **50g mooli, finely chopped**
— **200g cooked Japanese rice**
— **2 tbsp light soy sauce**
— **pinch of sea salt**
— **1 tsp mixed sesame seeds**
— **1 tsp grated root ginger**

Soak the shiitake mushrooms in 1 litre of warm water for 20 minutes, then strain into a bowl, pressing down on the mushrooms with a spoon and reserving the soaking liquid.

Add all the vegetables and mushrooms to a large saucepan, pouring in 500ml of the shiitake soaking liquid (discard the gritty bit at the bottom). Set over a medium heat and cook at a simmer for 15–20 minutes, until the carrots and mooli have softened.

Add the rice and return the broth to the simmer for two minutes.

Season with the soy sauce and salt, then ladle into bowls, sprinkling the sesame seeds and ginger on top.

SHABU SHABU

Use a medium casserole dish for this. The sauce here is thicker than the other Shabu shabu dressing in this book (see page 20). If you want a sauce that is more like a light dressing, do feel free to use that version instead. This one, though, is good to have with the recipe when you are also going to be drinking alcohol, at a party, say. It is meant as a feasting dish, so do feel free to scale up the quantities if you want. Tobanjan is a spicy paste; you can find it in Asian shops or online and you really need it in this sauce.

Serves 2–3

— 1 leek, sliced into julienne
— 1 whole lettuce, ripped into bite-sized pieces
— 400g wafer-thin sliced beef
  (shabu shabu beef)

For the sauce
— 1 tbsp brown sugar
— 1 tsp grated root ginger
— 1 tsp grated garlic
— ½ tbsp sesame oil
— ½ tbsp tobanjan
— 1 tbsp rice vinegar
— 1 tbsp soy sauce
— 1 tbsp white sesame seeds, crushed
  (see page 19)
— 50ml oyster sauce

First make the sauce. Dissolve the sugar in 3 tbsp of hot water in a bowl, then add all the other ingredients.

Pour 1.2 litres of water into a pan and bring to the boil. Reduce the heat to a simmer and add the leek. Cover and cook for two minutes.

Add the lettuce and three or four slices of beef, moving the beef around in the hot liquid with chopsticks and removing it once it's cooked. Skim any residue that appears on the surface of the water.

Serve the beef in small serving bowls, adding the lettuce and leek. Serve with the sauce.

STEAM AND MICROWAVE

"Learn the art of steaming food
and you will get maximum nutrition
from everything you cook."

Steaming is a beautifully gentle way of cooking, which is why I choose it for so many of my recipes. It's a really popular way to prepare food in Japan. Because this cooking method doesn't require any fussing with — stirring, flipping or the like — it is particularly suited to fragile foods such as fish, which can break up easily. Vegetables, which have a tendency to become soggy when boiled, also fare much better with steam cooking, retaining more of their colour and crispness. All of the Shoku-Iku goodness is preserved in steaming, as the food isn't submerged in liquid and therefore retains more of its nutrients. It's also a speedy way of cooking, as it takes only a short time to bring the steaming liquid up to temperature, unlike oven cooking where the oven can take time to heat up.

Steaming also keeps food succulently moist and incredibly fresh tasting. Besides cooking the food, the steam itself allows me to infuse flavours into whatever I am preparing.

I always line my steamer bowls with circles of baking parchment to make it easy to lift the food off once it is cooked. If I'm using an open-topped container as a steaming basket, I cover the top with a piece of muslin while the food cooks. This absorbs excess moisture, unlike a solid lid where the steam can collect and drip back on to the food.

You can use a microwave oven to produce a similar effect to steaming. Tightly cling film-wrap the items you want to cook before placing them in the microwave. This seals in the natural moisture and steam coming from the food and intensifies the flavours.

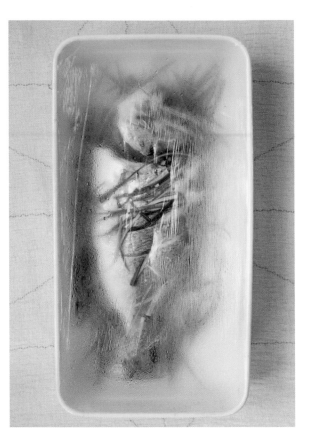

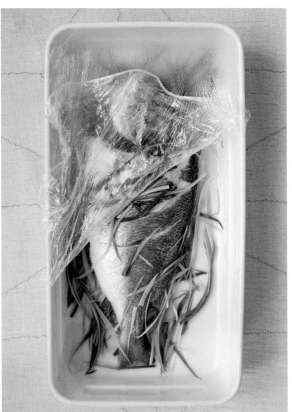
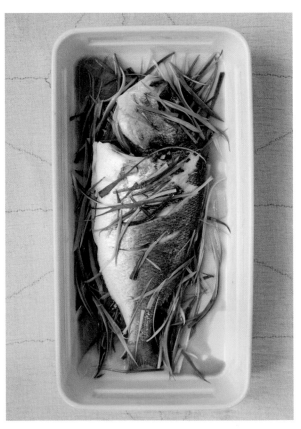

HEAVENLY STEAMED SEA BREAM

In Japan, and in some other food cultures, you sprinkle fish with sake and salt to get rid of 'fishy' flavours and to improve the texture.

Serves 2

— ½ leek, sliced into julienne
— 1 sea bream, skin slashed on both sides
— 2 tbsp sake
— pinch of sea salt
— 1 quantity Lemon soy sauce dressing
    (see page 20)

Place the leek and sea bream on a microwaveable dish. Sprinkle the sake and sea salt over both sides of the fish. Cover with cling film, making sure it is well sealed.

Using a 800w oven, microwave for four or five minutes, until done. Open carefully, being careful not to scald your hands in the steam.

Transfer to a serving plate and serve with the Lemon soy sauce dressing.

GLUTEN-FREE CHICKEN SAUSAGES

Both my son and my daughter are gluten-intolerant. They love sausages, but most that you can buy contain gluten, so I started to make these at home and they go down a storm.

Serves 2–3

— 2 skinless chicken breasts
— pinch of sea salt and freshly ground
    black pepper
— 30g grated onion
— 1 egg, lightly beaten
— 1 tbsp cornflour
— handful of rocket leaves
— 1 quantity Perfect with beer sauce
    (see page 20)

Mince one of the chicken breasts in a blender or food processor. Slice the other chicken breast in half horizontally across its width and open it out.

Place a 25cm length of cling film on the work top and lay the opened chicken breast on top. Season it.

Mix the minced chicken with all the other ingredients except the rocket and Perfect with beer sauce and place the mixture on the chicken breast.

Roll the chicken breast, wrapping cling film around it so it looks like a cracker. Wrap in foil.

Set up a steamer and place the chicken sausage inside. Steam for 10–12 minutes. Leave it to cool down, then remove the foil and cling film and slice into bite-sized pieces. Serve with rocket and Perfect with beer sauce.

SPICY STEAMED CHICKEN SALAD

Tobanjan is a spice blend. It's very hot and you don't need a lot; even a small amount really does have quite a kick. Serve this chicken with a salad of shredded lettuce, cucumber and spring onion.

Serves 2

For the sauce
— 2 tbsp soy sauce
— 1 tbsp mirin
— 1 tbsp caster sugar
— 2 tbsp sake
— 1 tsp tobanjan
— 1 tsp grated garlic
— 1 tbsp white sesame seeds, crushed
  (see page 19)

For the chicken
— 300–350g skinless boneless chicken thighs
— pinch of sea salt
— 2 tbsp sake
— 1 spring onion, cut into 10cm strips

Mix all the ingredients for the sauce together in a large bowl.

Slice the chicken thighs horizontally to make them thinner and season with sea salt on both sides.

Place the chicken in a dish and add the sake and spring onion. Turn to coat the chicken with the marinade, then set aside for 10 minutes.

Put the marinated chicken on a microwaveable tray, add the sauce and turn to coat again.

Wrap cling film around the tray and seal it well. Using a 800w oven, microwave for five minutes, then carefully open the cling film (be careful not to scald your hands in the steam) and turn the contents over.

Seal with cling film again and cook for another two to three minutes. Allow to cool to room temperature, then slice and serve with salad.

POSH DINNER IN 20 MINUTES

You can add a very little shredded sage to this, if you like. The cod is beautifully soft after steaming.

Serves 2

— 2 x 120g cod fillets
— 2 tbsp sake or white wine
— 4 cabbage leaves, in 1cm slices
— 30g carrot, finely sliced
— 4 frozen scallops, defrosted
— 2 tbsp grapeseed oil
— 1 tsp yuzu juice or lemon juice
— pinch of sea salt
— 1 quantity Everyday soy sauce dressing
  (see page 19)

Put the cod on a microwaveable tray and sprinkle with the sake. Leave for 15 minutes, then pat dry with kitchen paper.

Add the cabbage and carrot to the tray and sit the cod on top. Put the scallops on top of this and drizzle everything with the grapeseed oil and yuzu juice, sprinkling sea salt on top.

Cover with cling film. Using a 800w oven, microwave for four minutes, then leave, still wrapped in cling film, for another four minutes. Carefully unwrap (be careful not to scald your hands in the steam).

Serve with Everyday soy sauce dressing.

GINGER CHICKEN WITH BEANSPROUTS

This is incredibly easy to make — anybody could tackle it — and very delicious.

Serves 2–3

— 300g skinless boneless chicken thighs, cut into bite-sized pieces
— ½ onion, grated
— 1 garlic clove, finely sliced
— ½ thumb of root ginger, finely grated
— 6 tbsp sake or white wine
— 2 tbsp soy sauce
— pinch of freshly ground black pepper
— large handful of beansprouts
— 3–4 coriander leaves

Put the chicken in a plastic food bag with all the other ingredients except the beansprouts and coriander. Massage to cover the meat with all the flavourings and leave in the fridge for one hour.

Place a non-stick frying pan over a medium heat and empty in the chicken and sauce. Cook until the chicken is browned, then add the beansprouts, cover and steam for a final three or four minutes. Serve sprinkled with the coriander.

PRAWN PILLOW

This is very nice, with lots of lovely textures. It's essentially a very easy home-made dumpling. This is gluten-free as I use rice paper wrappers instead of wheat-based spring roll wrappers. I first made these for my gluten-free son and he loves them.

Makes 10

— 200g minced turkey or chicken
— 15cm length of leek, very finely chopped
— 1½ tbsp sake
— ½ tsp sea salt
— pinch of freshly ground black pepper
— 10 large rice paper sheets
— 20 large cooked prawns, deveined if necessary
— couple of handfuls of frozen edamame beans, defrosted
— 1 quantity Everyday soy sauce dressing or Lemon soy sauce dressing (see pages 19 and 20)

Put the minced turkey, leek, sake, sea salt and pepper into a bowl and mix well.

Place a rice paper sheet in a shallow dish of warm water for 10–15 seconds, to soften. Shake it gently to get rid of excess water and place on a large plate.

Spoon 1 tbsp of the turkey mixture on to the middle of the sheet and add two prawns and a few edamame beans. Fold it into a square as if you were wrapping a present. Repeat to use all the filling and rice papers.

Line a steamer with baking parchment. Place all the prawn pillows next to each other in the steamer, making sure the parcels do not touch.

Steam for five to six minutes, or until the parcels themselves are steaming.

Take out of the steamer and serve with your choice of soy sauce dressing.

STUFFED VEGETABLES

This is full of protein from the beans. When we have dishes that contain lots of protein but no meat, we call it 'meat of the garden'! But, if you do want some meat, this dish is nice with pork. It's also a good dish for sneaking lots of vegetables into recalcitrant children.

Serves 4

For the peppers and filling
— 2 tomatoes
— 1 aubergine, cut into 1cm cubes and soaked in water for 30 minutes
— 400g can soy beans or black eyed beans, drained and rinsed
— sea salt and freshly ground black pepper
— 1 green chilli, deseeded and finely chopped
— 2 green peppers, tops cut off
— 2 red peppers, tops cut off
— 1 quantity Shabu shabu dressing, (see page 20)

For the paste
— 1 tsp white miso paste
— 1 tbsp mirin
— 1 tbsp sake

Cut a cross at the base of tomatoes and put them in a bowl of boiling water for one minute. Remove, peel off the skin and cut into 1cm cubes.

Preheat the grill on its highest setting. Drain the aubergine and grill both aubergine and tomatoes on both sides for two to three minutes until lightly brown. Mix with the beans.

Mix together all the ingredients for the paste and stir into the aubergine mixture, seasoning to taste and adding the chilli.

Place the mixture into the peppers. Put on a large microwaveable tray and seal with cling film. Using a 800w oven, microwave for four minutes then leave, still covered with the cling film, for two minutes. Unwrap, being careful not to scald your hands.

If you would like a chargrilled finish, pop them under a hot grill until burnished. Serve with Shabu shabu dressing.

BRITISH PORK DUMPLINGS

I've called this recipe 'British' because it mixes apple with the pork filling. My children love the combination, so I invented this dumpling and it was a big hit.

Makes 20

For the filling
— 200g minced pork
— ½ medium onion, finely chopped
— 2 cabbage leaves, finely chopped
— ½ apple, peeled and grated
— 1 tbsp caster sugar
— 1 tbsp sesame oil
— 1 tbsp grated root ginger
— 1 tbsp sake
— 1 tbsp light soy sauce
— 1 tbsp cornflour

For the dumplings
— 20 wonton sheets
— 1 tsp cornflour
— 20 green peas
— a little flavourless vegetable oil, to brush
— 1 quantity Everyday soy sauce dressing or Shabu shabu dressing (see pages 19 and 20)

Mix all the filling ingredients, except the cornflour, in a bowl and set aside for 10 minutes. Add the cornflour and mix well again.

Hold a wonton sheet in your hand and put 1–1½ tbsp of filling into the centre of the sheet. Mix the 1 tsp of cornflour in a cup with 5 tbsp of water. Use this paste to moisten the sheet around the filling. Close your hand to mold the wonton into a ball shape, leaving the top open to expose the filling.

Push one green pea into the top of the filling.

Line a steamer with baking parchment. Brush a little oil under each dumpling and place them in the steamer, making sure they don't touch each other. Put the lid on and steam for five to seven minutes until cooked.

Serve with Shabu shabu dressing or Everyday soy sauce dressing.

BACON AND CABBAGE STEAMED PUDDING

You need to make this in a bowl, so you can build up a round shape; it should be like a cake or a pudding that you can cut into wedges to serve.

Serves 2–3

— **10 cabbage leaves, ribs removed**
— **10 rashers of unsmoked bacon**

Begin layering the cabbage and bacon in a medium microwaveable bowl. Start with a cabbage leaf first. Fill to the top. Push everything down to make sure it is tightly pressed together.

Cling film the top to seal it well.

Using a 800w oven, microwave for three to four minutes, until the bacon is cooked. Leave the bowl with the cling film still on for another five minutes.

Remove the cling film (be careful not to scald your hands in the steam) and place a large plate upside down on top of the bowl.

Tip over on to the plate and leave it for few seconds to make sure the cabbage and bacon are released. Cut like a cake to serve.

'FULL JAPANESE' GARDEN BREAKFAST

This is a quick, easy way of having eggs for breakfast. I always like to eat some greens at breakfast as well, as did all my family before me. This is a fusion of British and Japanese cooking methods and flavours —why not? I'm Japanese and I live in Britain—so I call it a 'full Japanese'. Use a lidded sauté pan.

Serves 2

— **1 tsp rapeseed oil**
— **1 garlic clove, grated**
— **large handful of kale, chopped into 1cm slices**
— **handful of baby spinach leaves**
— **3 cherry tomatoes, quartered**
— **3 shiitake mushrooms, finely sliced**
— **3 regular mushrooms, finely sliced**
— **4 eggs**
— **1 quantity Garden soy sauce dressing**
  (see page 20)
— **finely chopped chilli** (optional)

Heat the oil in a sauté pan over a medium heat, add the garlic and stir until fragrant.

Add the kale with any water from washing still clinging to its leaves, the spinach, tomatoes and mushrooms and cook until almost tender.

Hollow out four spaces and drop an egg into each. Put the lid on and cook over a low heat to steam for three to four minutes, depending on how you like your eggs (we only cooked two for the photo).

Transfer to plates and serve with Garden soy sauce dressing, sprinkled with chilli, if you want.

PUMPKIN OF PLENTY!

This is a Japanese monk vegan recipe. It is rich in umami and utterly delicious, with the soft, sweet pumpkin and tofu, but with a fresh, simple flavour. Use a round green squash with bright orange insides: Crown Prince is good.

Serves 3-4

— 1 small pumpkin, about 15cm in diameter
— 1 tbsp sesame oil
— 30g carrot, cut into 1cm strips
— 2 shiitake mushrooms, finely sliced
— 20g frozen edamame beans, defrosted
— sea salt
— 350g block of firm tofu, drained and dried with kitchen paper
— 2 tbsp white sesame seeds, crushed (see page 19)
— 1 tbsp cornflour

Sauce
— 400ml Basic dashi (see page 18)
— 2 tbsp mirin
— 2 tbsp light soy sauce
— 2 tbsp cornflour

Cut a 3cm lid off the top of the pumpkin. Deseed the inside of the pumpkin.

In a large steamer, steam the whole pumpkin with its lid for 15 minutes.

Meanwhile, heat a pan over a medium heat and add the sesame oil. Stir-fry the carrot, mushrooms and edamame for three minutes, seasoning with sea salt. Break the tofu into chunks and add them, too.

Add the crushed sesame and cornflour and mix well until the carrots soften.

Spoon the tofu and vegetable mix into the pumpkin and steam for another 10 minutes.

Meanwhile, heat a pan over a medium heat and add the dashi, mirin and soy sauce. Separately mix the cornflour with 5 tbsp of water, add to the pan and stir well until it thickens.

Remove the pumpkin lid and tip in the sauce. Serve.

CHICKEN LEMON POT

This steamed dish is very healthy and, like most steamed dishes, retains a lot of its nutrition. The flavour is very fresh and energising.

Serves 3-4

— 800g mooli, peeled and grated
— 5 leaves of Chinese leaf, cut into 5cm slices
— 500g skinless boneless chicken thighs, sliced 1cm thick
— 1 lemon, in 3mm slices
— 1 tbsp dashi flakes (or 50ml Motoko dashi, see page 18)
— 1 quantity Everyday soy sauce dressing or Lemon soy sauce dressing (see pages 19 and 20)

Lay the grated mooli in an even layer in a cast-iron saucepan or casserole dish. Lay the Chinese leaf, chicken and lemon on top, in that order.

Add the dashi flakes or Motoko dashi.

Cover and set the saucepan over a medium heat for six to seven minutes, or until you see steam coming out, then reduce the heat to low and cook for another four or five minutes. Turn the heat off completely and leave for a final five minutes.

Serve with your choice of soy sauce dressing.

MOOLI STEAK

Steamed mooli has quite a bland taste, subtler than
that of western radishes. This makes a main meal
when served with miso soup.

Serves 2

— **350g mooli, peeled and cut into 2cm slices**
— **1 quantity Perfect with beer sauce**
  (see page 20)

Place the mooli slices in a microwaveable tray,
next to each other but not on top of each other.
Add 2 tbsp of water and seal with cling film.

Using a 800w oven, microwave for five to seven
minutes then leave, still covered, for a further
three minutes. Unwrap, being careful not to scald
your hands in the steam.

Serve with Perfect with beer sauce.

STEAMED STICKY RICE

If I'm making this at home with my children, I need
to double the recipe, because they love it so much.
It is pretty addictive... Leave out the chicken for
a vegetarian version.

Serves 4–6

— **1 tbsp rapeseed oil**
— **100g skinless boneless chicken thighs,
  cut into 1cm cubes** (optional)
— **4 shiitake mushrooms, finely sliced**
— **60g carrots, sliced into julienne**
— **50g frozen burdock root, finely sliced
  or shredded**
— **4 oyster mushrooms, finely sliced**
— **1 head of enoki mushrooms, broken
  into pieces**
— **4 tbsp sake**
— **3 tbsp light soy sauce**
— **3 tbsp mirin**
— **1 tbsp caster sugar**
— **2 tbsp kelp flakes**
— **450g Japanese glutinous rice** (mochigome)
— **1 spring onion, finely chopped** (optional)
— **sprinkling of white sesame seeds** (optional)

Heat the rapeseed oil in a sauté pan set over
a medium heat and cook the chicken (if using),
turning, until lightly brown.

Add all the vegetables and seasonings and continue
to cook, stirring well, until the vegetables are tender.

Meanwhile, line a steamer with a muslin cloth, add the
rice and steam over a high heat for 30–35 minutes.

When the rice is ready, put it in a bowl with the
vegetables and mix well.

Return the mixture to the cloth-lined steamer and
cook for another 15 minutes over a high heat. Now
turn off the heat and leave, still covered, for a final
10 minutes. Serve sprinkled with either spring onion
or sesame seeds.

HOT STEAMED CHICKEN

This is very light, super-easy to make and has an authentically Asian taste to it. It's a typical dish you might see at a Japanese dinner table.

Serves 2–3

— **500g skinless boneless chicken thighs, cut into 1.5cm pieces**
— **1 tbsp sea salt**
— **2 tbsp sesame oil**
— **2 tbsp cornflour**
— **1 tbsp chicken stock**
— **1 tbsp soy sauce**
— **1 tbsp sake**
— **1 tbsp oyster sauce**
— **1 garlic clove, finely chopped**
— **1 spring onion, finely chopped**

Put the chicken in a bowl and add the sea salt and sesame oil. Stir so all the meat is coated and leave to marinate for 15 minutes. Stir in the cornflour.

Pour 150ml of water into a saucepan and add the stock, soy sauce, sake and oyster sauce. Bring to the boil, then remove from the heat.

Set up a steamer. Put the chicken into a heatproof dish and add the sauce. Sprinkle evenly with the garlic and steam for 20 minutes. Sprinkle with spring onion and serve.

JAPANESE GARDEN (gluten-free)

This dish was originally a Japanese monk recipe, a vegan dish. I tweaked it... and added bacon! I'm not sure the monks would approve. You can, of course, leave out the bacon.

Serves 2–3

— **200g pumpkin, cut into 1cm pieces**
— **200g turnips, quartered if large, left whole if tiny**
— **150g mooli, cut into 1cm half moons**
— **3 rashers of bacon**
— **200g broccoli, cut into 2cm pieces**
— **100g sugar snap peas**

For the sauce
— **2 tbsp balsamic vinegar**
— **1 tsp honey**
— **1 tbsp soy sauce**
— **1 tsp sesame oil**
— **1 tsp white sesame seeds, crushed** (see page 19)
— **pinch of sea salt**

Place the pumpkin, turnips and mooli into a large steamer, cover the top with bacon rashers and cook for six minutes.

Add the broccoli and sugar snap peas and cook for another three minutes.

Meanwhile, mix all the ingredients for the sauce.

Transfer the vegetables and bacon to a serving plate and sprinkle over the sauce.

JAPANESE SOUFFLÉ

The texture of this is soft, much softer than a western soufflé. You will need two medium-sized china cups. There's a bit of everything in this version, but leave out the chicken and prawns if you prefer.

Serves 2

— **500ml Basic dashi** (see page 18)
— **1 tbsp mirin**
— **½ tsp soy sauce**
— **1 tsp sea salt**
— **3 eggs, lightly beaten**
— **50g chicken breast, cut into 1cm pieces**
— **2–3 shiitake mushrooms, finely sliced**
— **2 small cooked prawns, deveined if necessary**
— **4 coriander leaves**

Pour the dashi, mirin and soy sauce in a bowl, add the salt and mix well. Add the eggs, then strain through a sieve to make sure the mixture is smooth.

Divide the chicken, mushrooms and prawns between two china cups and add the egg mixture; it should fill each cup by about two-thirds.

Place the cups in a steamer set over a medium heat and cook for 10 minutes, then reduce the heat to low and steam for another 10 minutes. Turn the heat off. Leave the cups in the steamer for a final five minutes. (If you don't have a steamer, place the cups in a deep saucepan containing 2cm of boiling water and cook, using the same timings.)

Sprinkle each cup with coriander and serve warm.

SWEET SOY SAUCE MOCHI

Mochi (pronounced 'mow-chee') is an authentic, classic Japanese dessert. The texture inside is very soft, almost silky.

Serves 4

For the mochi
— **150g rice flour**

For the sauce
— **2 tbsp soy sauce**
— **2 tbsp caster sugar**
— **1 tbsp cornflour**

Soak four bamboo skewers in a dish of water.

Put the rice flour into a large bowl and gradually pour in 150ml of warm water, stirring with a wooden spoon. Knead the dough with your hands for two to three minutes.

Lay a damp cloth into a steamer.

Cut the mochi dough into 2cm balls — or any shapes really — and lay them on top, then steam over a high heat for 15 minutes. This is just to cook the mixture through and they won't remain in the shapes they hold at this stage, so don't waste time shaping them!

Remove the mochi balls from the steamer and place on a sheet of greaseproof paper. Hold the sides of the greaseproof paper, bringing the dough balls together. Massage through the paper well until the dough feels soft and fleshy. Cut the mass into 12 pieces, roll each into a ball and put three balls on each skewer.

Preheat the grill on its highest setting. Put foil around the exposed parts of the skewers and grill each on both sides for two minutes.

Meanwhile, make the sauce. Put all the ingredients into a small saucepan with 100ml of water and cook over a medium heat. When it's bubbling, mix well with a wooden spoon, turning the heat off once it has become clearer and thicker.

Serve on top of the mochi.

SWEET POTATO TREAT

You can eat this as a snack, a dessert or a side dish. You can also cool the mixture and wrap it in puff pastry, forming a triangle of pastry around the filling. You could cook that under a medium grill, turning to cook both sides. Though delicious that, of course, would be far less Shoku-Iku and far more western...

Serves 3–4

— **400g sweet potato, peeled and cut into 5mm slices**
— **2 apples, peeled and cut into 1cm slices**
— **80ml sake**
— **25g honey**
— **1½ tsp sea salt**

Place the sweet potato slices in a saucepan, laying them next to each other, then place the apple slices on top.

Pour in 200ml of water and add the sake, honey and sea salt. Set over a high heat and cook until you see steam coming out of the pan, then reduce the heat to medium and steam for another four to five minutes until all the liquid has been absorbed.

FRUIT BUNS

This is a great snack for lunch or between meals. I also put it in lunch boxes. It's really easy to make.

Makes 6–7

— **½ tsp sea salt**
— **1 tsp baking powder**
— **40g caster sugar**
— **150g plain flour** (or gluten-free flour)
— **5 peeled oranges, sliced**
— **2 apples, finely sliced**
— **10 raisins**

Pour 150ml of room temperature water into a bowl and add the salt, baking powder and sugar. Now stir in the flour.

Divide between six or seven 4cm-wide pudding tins, or heatproof muffin tins, arranging orange, apple and/or raisins on top on each.

Put the tins on a steamer rack, cover with a cloth instead of a lid, to absorb the water, then steam for 15 minutes.

GRILL AND FRY

"Intensify the natural flavours
of your food with the flashing
heat of a grill."

Grilling is such a clean way to cook, as it doesn't need to involve oils as frying does (even if you are frying a low-fat foodstuff, it will always pick up the oils from the pan). And of course when grilling, any excess fats in food will drip off, lowering its fatty content. In this chapter, 'grilling' can mean grilling under a heat source, or griddling in a pan.

Remember, when grilling or frying meats, to always allow a resting period. As tempting as the food may smell, let it sit for a few minutes. This allows the juices in the meat to permeate back through it and not flood out when cut. It also improves the texture, by allowing the fibres to relax and soften.

Grilling or frying also adds to the flavour of your food. Any natural sugars in vegetables will caramelise slightly, making them irresistible with very little effort. I use plenty of marinades when grilling and frying and again the taste is amplified, as the flavours heat and bubble under a hot grill or in a hot pan.

Cooking vegetables this way keeps more of the vitamins and nutrients than other cooking methods, such as boiling. I also find that my children are less resistant to vegetables when they are grilled or fried.

This chapter gives me a chance to experiment with things you wouldn't normally associate with grilling or frying. My Full of goodness recipe (see page 75) is incredibly speedy to make, though you are grilling pumpkin. The key is to slice the pumpkin nice and thinly so it becomes succulent under the grill quickly. My mother is a fan of lightly grilled avocado strips (see page 75). And of course you can toast nuts and seeds just as easily under the grill rather than fry them.

JAPANESE BURGER

This recipe is perfect for my three children. The tofu makes the burger light and more digestion-friendly, as it has soy protein rather than just all meat.

Makes 3–4 burgers

For the burgers
— 100g tofu
— 100g minced turkey
— 1 tsp grated garlic
— 1 egg, lightly beaten
— ½ onion, grated
— sea salt
— 100g chickpeas, mashed
— ½ tbsp sesame oil

For the bean salad
— 2 tbsp rapeseed oil
— 225g canned azuki beans, drained and rinsed
— 2 shallots, finely chopped
— 10 green beans, chopped into 5mm lengths
— 2 tomatoes, finely chopped
— 3 tbsp balsamic vinegar
— ½ tsp red chilli powder

To serve
— 30g mooli, grated (about 4 tbsp)
— 4 oba leaves, or coriander leaves, shredded
— ¼ lemon

Pat the tofu dry with kitchen paper, then place in a microwaveable bowl, seal with cling film and using a 800w oven, microwave for five minutes. Leave, covered, for another three minutes.

Add to a bowl with the turkey, garlic, egg, onion, sea salt and chickpeas and mix well. Leave it for 10 minutes to settle.

Take 100–120g of the mixture in your hands and shape it into a burger. Squeeze it lightly to make sure there is no air in the meat. Repeat to make three or four burgers.

Heat a non-stick pan over medium heat and add the sesame oil. Place the burgers into the pan and fry for three to four minutes on each side.

Add 2 tbsp water to the pan and put the lid on. Cook for another few minutes, until the water has gone.

Meanwhile, make the bean salad. Heat a pan over a medium heat and add the rapeseed oil. Add the azuki beans and shallots and fry until the shallots soften. Turn the heat off and let cool. (I usually take them out of the pan to cool.)

Put the green beans in a microwaveable tray and add 1 tbsp of water. Seal it well with cling film. Cook in the microwave for three minutes then leave, covered, for another three minutes. Remove from the tray and leave to cool.

Put the tomatoes in a bowl and add the green beans, azuki bean mixture, balsamic vinegar and chilli.

Mix the grated mooli and oba well. Serve the burger with grated mooli and oba on top, with a pile of bean salad. Squeeze a little bit of lemon juice on top of the mooli and serve.

PRAWN BARBECUE

These prawns have a great flavour balance between the lemon and the garlic. Despite containing no hot spices, this dish nevertheless gives a bit of a kick.

Serves 3

— 2 tbsp grapeseed oil
— 1 tbsp sake
— 1 tsp grated garlic
— 5 tbsp lemon juice, plus lemon wedges to serve (optional)
— ½ tsp freshly ground white pepper
— 1 tsp sea salt
— 15 tiger prawns, heads removed, shelled and deveined
— 5 spring onions, sliced into julienne

Put the grapeseed oil, sake, garlic, lemon juice, pepper and salt in a plastic food bag, add the prawns, close the bag and massage to coat. Leave for two hours in the fridge. If you want to serve them on bamboo skewers, soak the skewers for at least 30 minutes, so they don't catch fire in the pan.

When you're ready to cook, you can thread the prawns on to bamboo skewers. Otherwise just cook them as they are.

Place a large frying pan over a medium heat and allow to get hot. Add the prawns and their marinade and cook for two minutes on each side.

Transfer the prawns and sauce to a serving dish and sprinkle with the spring onions. Serve with lemon wedges, if you like.

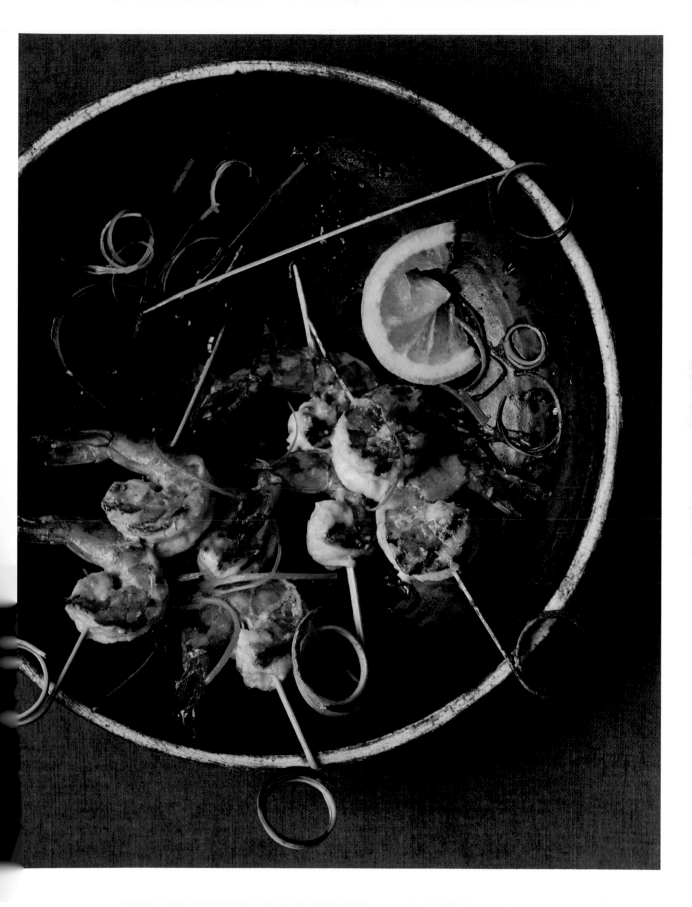

JAPANESE GRILLED VEGETABLE 'STIR-FRY'

This is a dish completely without oil, that is half-grilled and half-steamed to give satisfying umami flavours. You can taste the vegetables in it rather than just soy sauce, black bean sauce or oyster sauce, which can be the case in traditional stir-fries.

Serves 2

— 200g beansprouts
— 100g baby spinach
— 60–80g carrots, very finely sliced
— 4 asparagus spears, cut into 3cm pieces
— sea salt and freshly ground black pepper
— 1 quantity Everyday soy sauce dressing
  or Lemon soy sauce dressing
  (see pages 19 and 20)
— white sesame seeds, to serve

Place all the vegetables in a microwaveable tray, add 1 tbsp of water and seal with cling film.

Using a 800w oven, microwave for four minutes, then leave, covered, for another two minutes. Remove the cling film, being careful not to scald your hands.

Heat a frying or griddle pan on a high heat and grill the asparagus and carrots quickly without any oil until lightly browned on both sides. (This depends on how you like it. I like asparagus lightly charred.)

Put the beansprouts, spinach, carrots and asparagus in a bowl and mix well.

Season with sea salt and pepper. Serve with your choice of soy sauce dressing and sprinkle with white sesame seeds.

AUBERGINE AND SHALLOT SALAD

This could make a main dish or a side, depending on what you prefer.

Serves 2

— 7 small shallots, peeled and finely sliced
— 1 aubergine, cut into 4, then sliced into
  1mm pieces
— 2–3 tbsp Lemon soy sauce dressing
  (see page 20)

Soak the shallot slices in water for 10 minutes, then drain.

Preheat the grill on its highest setting. Put the aubergine in a grill pan and grill on both sides until it is brown.

Mix the aubergine and shallots well in a bowl and add the Lemon soy sauce dressing.

FULL OF GOODNESS

We eat this as a main dish. There are lots of different colours in it, which means you eat it with your eyes as well as with your palate.

Serves 2–3

For the vegetables
— **2 tomatoes, cut into 5mm slices**
— **1 courgette, cut into 5mm slices**
— **1 red pepper, cut into 5mm slices**
— **1 yellow pepper, cut into 5mm slices**
— **40g lotus root, cut into 5mm slices**
— **40g pumpkin, cut into 5mm slices**

For the sauce
— **30g bonito flakes**
— **2 tbsp soy sauce**
— **2 tbsp rice vinegar**
— **2 tbsp rapeseed or grapeseed oil**
— **pinch of sea salt**
— **pinch of caster sugar**

Preheat the grill on its highest setting, or heat a griddle pan. Place all the vegetables on a tray and grill both sides for three to four minutes, or for longer if you like a little smoky flavour. Or use the griddle pan if you want griddle marks.

Meanwhile, make the sauce. Pour 200ml of hot water into a cup and add the bonito flakes. Leave for five minutes. Add the rest of the ingredients and mix well.

Transfer the vegetables to a serving plate and pour over the sauce. Serve immediately.

GRILLED AVOCADO

The texture of a grilled avocado is creamy and sort of buttery. Me and my mum tried grilling avocado one day as an experiment. We wanted to see if you could use it for anything other than salads. And you can!

Serves 4 as a side dish

— **3 fingers of okra**
— **2 avocados**
— **4 cherry tomatoes, quartered**
— **sprinkling of dried seaweed**

For the sauce
— **7g bonito flakes**
— **2 umeboshi** (salted plums), **pitted and mashed**
— **½ tsp wasabi paste**
— **½ tsp soy sauce**
— **1 tsp mirin**

Boil the okra fingers for two minutes, until tender, then drain and cut into 5mm slices.

Preheat the grill on its highest setting. Cut the avocados in half, remove the stones, peel and slice. Grill, turning, until browned. Cut into cubes.

Put the avocados, okra and tomatoes in a bowl.

Separately mix all the ingredients for the sauce. Add the sauce to the vegetables and mix well.

Serve in small bowls and sprinkle seaweed on top.

CHILLI TOFU

You can eat this as a side dish or as a snack. I like to eat it with rice, but westerners may find it a bit dry that way.

Serves 2

— **350g block of tofu, cut into 2cm cubes**
— **½ leek, cut into 1cm slices**
— **6 dried red chillies**

For the sauce
— **2 tbsp white miso**
— **2 tbsp sake**
— **1 tbsp soy sauce**
— **1 tsp caster sugar**
— **2 tbsp balsamic vinegar**

Preheat the grill on its highest setting, or heat a griddle pan if you want to get griddle marks. Pat the tofu with kitchen paper to get rid of any water, then grill it and the leek on both sides for three minutes each, until brown. At the same time, grill the dried chillies for three minutes. This should be just enough to bring their flavours out, but don't blacken or scorch them. You can griddle all the components instead, if you prefer.

Meanwhile, make the sauce. Mix the miso with the sake and place into a small saucepan. Add the chillies and cook for a few minutes until flavoured.

Add the soy sauce, sugar and 50ml of water and bring to a simmer. Once it's boiling, reduce the heat to low and add the balsamic vinegar.

Add the tofu and leek and cook over a low heat for 15–20 minutes until the liquid has been absorbed.

MUSTARD CHICKEN

A more westernised dish, even though my Japanese dad invented it! It's great for summer eating.

Serves 2

— **300g skin-on boneless chicken thighs, cut into 2cm strips**
— **sprinkling of sake**
— **½ onion, grated**
— **pinch of sea salt and freshly ground black pepper**

For the marinade
— **½ tsp grated garlic**
— **1 tsp soy sauce**
— **2 tsp brown sugar**
— **1 tbsp French mustard**
— **½ tbsp English mustard**

Lay the chicken on a tray and sprinkle with sake. Stir in the onion and some seasoning. Set aside to marinate for 10 minutes. Preheat the grill on its highest setting.

Transfer the chicken to a grill tray or baking sheet and grill both side for four to five minutes. Once it is nice and brown, put it in a bowl with the marinade ingredients and mix well.

Return the chicken to the tray and grill for another few minutes.

Serve with shredded lettuce and finely sliced onions.

GRILLED SPRING ROLLS

Instead of frying spring rolls, in the usual manner, these grilled versions are low in oil and (of course) calories, but are nevertheless wonderfully crisp.

Makes 6–7

— **350g pork, cut into wafer-thin slices**
— **1 tbsp sake**
— **1 tsp soy sauce**
— **100g shiitake mushrooms, finely sliced**
— **50g bamboo** (canned is fine), **finely sliced**
— **2 spring onions, cut into 10cm strips**
— **1 thumb of root ginger, finely sliced**
— **handful of coriander leaves and stalks**
— **1 tsp sesame oil**
— **1 tbsp cornflour**
— **6–7 spring roll sheets**

Mix the pork with the sake and soy sauce, cover and leave to marinate for 20 minutes.

Put the pork, mushrooms, bamboo, spring onions, ginger, coriander and sesame oil in a bowl and mix well with your hands.

Mix the cornflour with enough water to make a smooth paste (you will be using it as a 'glue').

Place a spring roll sheet on a work surface. Put a handful of the pork mixture in the centre of the sheet.

Fold over two opposite corners (left and right) of the spring roll sheet just to cover the ends of the filling, then roll from the bottom to the top of the sheet, brushing the cornflour mixture around the edges to seal it well. Repeat to use up all the filling and spring roll sheets.

Keep the rolls on a tray, sealed sides down. Preheat the grill on its medium setting, or heat a griddle pan. Grill or griddle for 10 minutes each, turning, until nicely bronzed.

MAKI'S COD MISO

This has a nice soft and melting texture and quite
a strong miso flavour. With the Shoku-Iku style of
eating, a few dishes should be arranged together,
so you might eat this fish with miso soup with tofu
and seaweed, pickles, or rice, as in the photo. Let
the power of five (see pages 7–15) inform your
choices: you should aim for a good mixture of food
groups, textures, colours and cooking methods.

Serves 4

For the fish
— **4 x 120g fillets of cod**
   (fresh is better than frozen for this)
— **pinch of sea salt**
— **3 tbsp sake**
— **40g mooli, grated**

For the paste
— **3 tbsp mirin**
— **4 tbsp sake**
— **300g white miso**

Lay the cod on a tray and sprinkle with the sea salt
and sake. Set aside for 10 minutes.

Mix all the ingredients for the paste.

Smooth half the paste on to a small tray which can fit
all the cod in a single layer. Place the cod on top and
coat with the rest of the paste, covering completely.
Seal with cling film and leave in the fridge overnight.

Next day, scrape any excess paste from the cod.
Preheat the grill on a medium setting. Grill the cod
for 10 minutes until lightly brown. Cover with foil
and leave it for another three minutes.

Serve with the mooli.

MAKI'S MISO PORK

I usually marinate this before I go to bed to cook
the next day. Serve with steamed broccoli and rice.

Serves 2–3

— **2 pork fillets (400–500g), sliced into
   5mm slices**
— **2 tbsp white miso**
— **1 tbsp sake or white wine**
— **1 tsp honey**
— **1 tsp soy sauce**
— **1 tsp mirin**
— **2 tsp sesame oil**
— **1 tsp grated garlic**
— **1 orange, peeled and sliced**
— **2 handfuls of salad leaves**

Put the pork in a plastic food bag and add all the
other ingredients except the orange and salad leaves.
Seal the bag, while pushing out all the air you can,
then massage it for one minute to really help the
marinade to penetrate the meat. Leave the bag in the
fridge overnight.

Preheat the grill on its highest setting, or heat
a griddle pan. Lightly grill or griddle both sides
of the pork until it is dark brown, then serve with
the orange slices and leaves.

MAKI'S RICE CRACKERS

These are meant as a between-meal snack
or for lunch boxes.

Makes 2

— **120–150g cooked Japanese glutinous rice**
  (see page 110), **warm or cold**
— **½ tsp sesame oil**
— **1 tbsp mirin**
— **1 tbsp soy sauce**

Lay a 30cm-long sheet of greaseproof paper on
a work top and put half the rice in the middle. Fold
the paper in half and flatten the pile of rice until it
is 5mm thick. Repeat with the other half of the rice.

Heat a pan over a medium heat with the sesame oil.

Fry the rice patties on both side for two minutes while
you separately mix together the mirin and soy sauces.
Brush the rice patties with the sauce and turn,
repeating this brushing and turning three to four
times until brown.

Serve immediately, or cover the pan and reheat the
crackers when required.

SWEET POTATO DREAM

You can put carrots in this as well if you want to hide
them! It's beautifully sweet and they will slip down
unnoticed. This is a very authentic dessert or snack,
great to eat instead of any cakes containing wheat
or flour. Another one good for lunch boxes.

Serves 4 / Makes 10–12

— **300g sweet potato, peeled and cut into
  1cm cubes**
— **30g brown sugar**
— **10g honey**
— **1 egg yolk, lightly beaten**

Place the sweet potato in a microwaveable tray and
cover with cling film. Microwave for six minutes.

Once the potato is soft, add the sugar and mash well.
Add the honey and stir until smooth.

Hold a 20cm-wide piece of cling film on your hand
and place 2 tbsp of potato mix in the centre. Close
your hand, shaping the mix like an egg.

Preheat the grill on its highest setting. Unwrap the
potato mix and brush the beaten egg yolk all over.
Grill for three minutes, turning, or until brown on
all sides.

Serve warm or cold.

NO-COOK

"Turn off your oven and discover
a whole new way to prepare food."

Japanese cuisine is famous for raw fish and it's hardly surprising that many of my recipes require absolutely no heat or cooking. There are some previously cooked foods in this chapter — such as prawns and tofu — but not many. And you don't have to cook them yourself. For me, the benefits of no-cooking are plentiful.

First and foremost, raw foods sum up the Shoku-Iku ethos of goodness, nutrition and conscious eating, as there is no surer way to preserve a food's integrity and goodness. I also find that, when eating raw foods, it's natural that you would select variety. For instance, my salads are made from numerous vegetables and herbs and not just from green leaves. This chapter also illustrates how raw foods can be made extra tasty simply with the addition of other raw ingredients, which have been pickled instead of cooked to intensify their flavours.

Raw foods contain far higher levels of nutrients than cooked foods; some nutritionists believe up to one-third more. Without the effects of cooking, foods also retain far higher levels of fibre. Raw food exercises our gums and jaws as we chew it, boosts the immune system and brightens our skin, especially if you include seeds and nuts in the mix.

Fresh and raw food also looks so beautiful. The colours of natural uncooked foods are so vibrant and appealing. Once you get into the habit of incorporating raw foods into your daily diet, a plate of cooked food can look dull beside them. Because raw food retains its natural moisture content it helps you to feel full but not as though you have overeaten. Once you start consciously mixing raw dishes into your daily meals, you won't look back.

VINEGARED PRAWN SALAD

This is a lovely side dish, with piquant, satisfying
flavours. The dried seaweed you need here is the
shredded type, in packets.

Serves 2–3

— 40g dried seaweed
— 1 cucumber, sliced into julienne
— 6 cooked, peeled prawns, deveined
  if necessary

For the dressing
— 1/3 tsp sea salt
— 2 tbsp rice vinegar
— 2 tbsp caster sugar or honey
— 1 tsp white sesame seeds
— 1 tsp soy sauce

Soak the seaweed in a bowl in one litre of water
for 20 minutes. Drain and squeeze to make sure
you remove all the water.

Meanwhile, put the salt, vinegar and sugar in a
separate bowl and mix until the sugar dissolves.
Add the sesame seeds and mix well.

Add the seaweed, cucumber and prawns to the
sauce and mix well. Cover and leave in the fridge
for 30 minutes. Serve, stirring in the soy sauce.

JAPANESE PICKLES

This side dish can be eaten with anything, or even
just with plain rice as a palate enlivener.

Makes 5–6 small servings

— **5 leaves of Chinese leaf, cut into 1cm slices**
— **1 whole cucumber, cut into 1cm slices**
— **2 white turnips, cut into 1cm slices,
   or 6–8 small turnips, quartered**
— **1 onion, cut into 5mm slices**

For the sauce
— **½ tsp white sesame seeds, crushed**
   (see page 19), **plus 1 tsp whole white
   sesame seeds**
— **2 tsp rice vinegar**
— **2 tsp soy sauce**
— **2 tsp sesame oil**

Pour all the ingredients for the sauce, except the
whole sesame seeds, into a plastic food bag and add
all the vegetables. Seal well and put it in the fridge
for one hour.

Drain all the liquid and serve in a small bowl with
the white sesame seeds sprinkled on top.

This will keep, covered, in the fridge for seven days.
If it throws off a lot of liquid in that time, simply drain
it off before using.

ICED TOMATO

These make a really refreshing mouthful and are perfect for summer; I can eat two or three at a time! They are really good with barbecued food.

Makes 4

— **4 medium tomatoes**

For the sauce
— **2 tbsp soy sauce**
— **1 tbsp mirin**
— **1 tsp caster sugar**
— **1 tsp sea salt**
— **800ml Basic dashi** (see page 18)

For the topping
— **5 oba leaves, or coriander leaves, shredded**
— **½ shallot, finely sliced**
— **½ thumb of root ginger, grated**

Peel the tomatoes (see page 53). Mix together all the ingredients for the sauce.

Coat the whole tomatoes with the sauce in a large bowl, then seal it with cling film. Chill in the fridge for one day.

Serve in a small bowl and sprinkle the oba, shallot and ginger on top.

SPINACH SALAD

Although you might think of this as a side dish or a light lunch, my mum actually eats it every morning at breakfast.She always wants to have greens at breakfast, to get as many in as she can. Shoku-Iku!

Serves 2 as a side dish

— **handful of baby spinach**
— **5 lettuce leaves, cut into 2cm strips**

For the dressing
— **1 tbsp honey**
— **2 tbsp Noodle soup stock** (see page 18)
— **1 tbsp white sesame seeds, crushed** (see page 19)
— **2 tbsp sesame oil**
— **1 sheet of dried nori, crumbled**

Mix together all the ingredients for the dressing.

Put the spinach and lettuce in a bowl and add the dressing. Stir together and serve.

CHICORY WITH COD'S ROE SALAD

You could serve this as a canapé or a very elegant starter. I first made it for a friend's wedding and it went down a treat. Obviously scale up the quantities to make more.

Makes 5

— 50g smoked cod's roe, very finely sliced
— 40g celery, finely sliced
— 5 chicory leaves
— 1 tsp rapeseed oil

Mix the cod's roe and celery in a bowl.

Place spoonfuls of the cod roe mixture on chicory leaves and sprinkle with rapeseed oil.

HONEY TOMATO WITH TOFU
Image on page 96

This is a kind of salad, and meant as a side dish. I prefer it with silken tofu, but it is also good with the firm kind, if you like. It is great with Hot steamed chicken and Mustard chicken (see pages 60 and 79).

Serves 3–4

— 1 large tomato, deseeded and cut into 1cm
  pieces (see page 53), or leave it chunky,
  if you prefer
— 1 large shallot, finely chopped
— 350g block of silken or firm tofu, cut into
  3 x 1cm batons, or cubes
— a few small coriander leaves

For the dressing
— 1 tbsp honey
— 1 tbsp balsamic vinegar
— 1 tbsp soy sauce

Put the tomato and shallot into a small bowl. Mix all the ingredients for the dressing and add to the bowl. Mix well and place in the fridge for 30 minutes.

Lay the tofu on a plate and place the tomato and shallots on top. Dress with the coriander leaves.

KALE SALAD

Image on page 97

You can eat this warm, though it is more usually
served cold. Kale has quite a strong flavour,
so you don't need a lot.

Serves 3–4 as a side dish

— **8 kale leaves, coarse ribs removed, cut into
  4cm strips**
— **1 tbsp white sesame seeds, crushed**
  (see page 19)
— **1 tbsp light soy sauce**
— **2 tbsp sesame oil**

Put the kale in a pan and add 50ml of water. Cover
and simmer for three to five minutes, or until tender.
Squeeze the liquid from the kale.

Place the kale in a serving bowl and add all the other
ingredients. Mix well and serve with meat dishes.

OKRA WITH CANNED TUNA

This is a kind of fusion dish, with western and
Japanese influences.

Serves 2 as a side dish

— **10 okra fingers, blanched for two minutes**
  (see page 75)
— **160g can of tuna in spring water, drained**

For the sauce
— **1 tsp lemon juice**
— **2 tsp French mustard**
— **½ tsp light soy sauce**

Cut each okra finger into pieces.

Put the tuna in a bowl. In a separate bowl,
mix together all the ingredients for the sauce.

Mix the tuna and sauce with the okra, turning to coat,
then serve straight away.

FIVE SENSES SUSHI

"People shouldn't be afraid of creating sushi. Don't worry about being too authentic, just enjoy the process. Here are some imaginative ways to get you started. Great tasting and great fun, too."

Sushi for me, with all its accompanying pastes and pickles, is one of the tastiest of foods and its soaring popularity in the west is testament to this.

If you have never thought about creating your own sushi, then start thinking! You only need some bamboo rolling mats, sushi or Japanese rice and a good bottle of rice vinegar. I find most people's resistance to making sushi at home comes from the mistaken idea that it will be too tricky to make. In fact it couldn't be simpler and, once you have perfected cooking good Japanese rice, it is barely more complicated than making a sandwich. I have taught thousands (literally) of people to make sushi and I always tell them what I will tell you now: as long as you enjoy the taste, it doesn't matter if at first it doesn't look perfectly neat. That comes with practice.

Sushi is a soothing meal, refreshing during hotter months, but also perfect as a meal following any over-indulgence as it doesn't sit heavily on the stomach. If you eat it for lunch, you won't feel weighed down as you tackle the afternoon's work.

The effect of eating sushi on your health and your senses is well documented: the omega-3 rich fish, the iron-boosting seaweed wrapper and the non-fat energy from rice. Even the pickled ginger has been found to aid digestion, while wasabi has been identified as having tooth-protective qualities as well as ensuring fresh breath.

The beauty and colours of sushi — as well as its nourishing and sense stimulating qualities — make it the epitome of Shoku-Iku foods.

AVOCADO AND PEAR QUINOA POWER SUSHI

I always wrap cling film around my sushi rolling mats before using, as this prevents the rice (or quinoa, in this case) from sticking at all. For a step-by-step guide to how to roll sushi, see page 21.

Serves 2–3

— **200g quinoa**
— **3 tbsp puréed or mashed mango**
  (mashed with a fork)
— **1 tsp white wine vinegar**
— **1 tsp lemon juice**
— **pinch of sea salt**
— **1 medium pear**
— **4–5 full sheets of dried nori seaweed**
— **1 avocado, finely sliced**

Place the quinoa into a sieve and rinse well under cold water. Tip the rinsed quinoa into a saucepan, add 400ml of water and cook over a medium heat.

Bring to the boil, then reduce the heat to a simmer. Cook for about 13 minutes until soft, stirring frequently. Drain well to remove any excess water.

Put the cooked quinoa in a bowl and let it cool to lukewarm for few minutes.

Add the mango purée, vinegar, lemon juice and sea salt to the quinoa while still warm and mix well. Transfer to a tray, spreading the quinoa thinly, and allow it to cool completely.

Meanwhile, preheat the grill. Finely slice the pear and grill the slices for two or three minutes on each side.

Place a nori sheet on a sushi rolling mat, long side towards you and rough side up, shiny side down. Spread one-quarter to one-fifth (depending on whether you are making four or five rolls) of the quinoa mix from the bottom to two-thirds of the way up the sheet.

Place 4 slices of avocado and 3 slices of lightly grilled pear along the middle of the quinoa. Roll the nori tightly up to the end. Leave it to sit for two to three minutes to allow the seaweed to soften.

Repeat to use up all the nori sheets, rice and filling.

Cut each roll into six pieces, then serve.

BROWN SUSHI RICE

I always cook brown rice in a pressure cooker, as I find it most convenient that way. It is hard to cook smaller quantities than this so, if you find you have too much for a recipe, freeze the rest. Never refrigerate it, as that will spoil the texture.

Makes enough for 2–3

— **400g brown sushi rice**
— **500ml cold water**
— **100ml sushi vinegar**

Rinse the rice quickly under cold water, then drain. Place the rice and measured water into a pressure cooker. Wait until it comes to the boil, then reduce the heat to low and cook for about 20 minutes.

Remove the lid quickly so the moisture doesn't drip down on to the rice.

Wait until the pressure cooker cools down, then transfer the hot rice to a shallow bowl.

Add the sushi vinegar and mix well. Spread it out thinly on a tray and let it cool to lukewarm.

BROWN SHIITAKE AND PUMPKIN SUSHI

Always season sushi rice with vinegar while it is still hot, so it soaks up all the flavours (see left). I designed this recipe to be rolled so the rice ends up on the outside, like a California roll, but you can roll it the more conventional way as well, as we did for the photo. For a step-by-step guide to how to roll both types, see page 21.

Serves 2–3

— **10 shiitake mushrooms, stems removed, finely sliced**
— **¼ pumpkin, finely sliced**
— **sea salt**
— **450g Brown sushi rice, cooked and seasoned with sushi vinegar, lukewarm** (see left)
— **3 half sheets of dried nori seaweed.**
— **handful of spinach leaves**

Preheat the grill on its highest setting, or heat a griddle pan. Grill the mushrooms and pumpkin, both sprinkled with sea salt, on both sides, until cooked.

Take about 150g of the rice and spread all over the rough side of a half sheet of nori on a rolling mat.

Flip the sheet upside down so the seaweed is on the top, facing you. The roll should still be on the mat.

Place one-third of the spinach, pumpkin and mushrooms in a row across the seaweed.

Roll, leaving the brown rice on the outside. Repeat with the other half sheets of nori and the remaining rice and filling.

Cut each roll into six pieces, then serve.

BROWN RICE TUNA SUSHI
WITH SWEET-HOT SAUCE

The sauce here is sweet and spicy and very moreish. A hugely satisfying dish. Again, you can choose to roll this in the conventional manner or as a California roll, as you prefer. For a step-by-step guide to how to roll both types, see page 21.

Serves 2–3

For the sauce
— 1 apple, peeled, cored and chopped
— 1 tbsp honey
— 1 tbsp mirin
— 1 tbsp wasabi powder
— 1 tbsp light soy sauce

For the sushi
— 100ml dry sake
— 100g sushi-grade tuna, sliced into batons
— 450g Brown sushi rice, cooked and seasoned
  with sushi vinegar, lukewarm (see page 104)
— 3 half sheets of dried nori seaweed

Put the apple, honey and mirin in a saucepan and cook for 15–20 minutes over a medium heat until the apple is soft. Put the apple mix in a blender and add the wasabi and soy sauce. Blend until smooth.

Pour the sake into a bowl and add the tuna. Leave to soak for 20–30 minutes.

Take about 150g of the rice and spread all over the rough side of a half sheet of nori on a rolling mat.

Flip the sheet upside down so the seaweed is on the top, facing you. It should still be on the mat.

Place one-third of the marinated tuna in a row across the seaweed. Then roll, leaving the brown rice on the outside. Repeat with the other half sheets of nori and the remaining rice and filling.

Cut each roll into six pieces, then serve, with the sauce on top or on the side.

WHITE SUSHI RICE

This may make more than you need for the recipes here, but it freezes really well in smaller portions once cooked. Never put cooked sushi rice in the fridge, as that will ruin its yielding texture.

Makes enough for 5–6

— **600ml white sushi rice**
   (best measured in a measuring jug)
— **660ml cold water**
— **120ml sushi vinegar**

Wash the rice thoroughly, then leave it to dry for at least 30 minutes in a sieve.

Find a large pan with a tight-fitting lid. I find a casserole dish better for cooking this rice than a regular saucepan.

Measure the water and put it in the pan. Tip in the rice. Place over a medium heat, cover and leave for 10–13 minutes, until it comes to the boil (listen for the bubbles; do not remove the lid).

When the water has come to the boil, reduce the heat to its lowest for 30 seconds, then turn the heat off. Leave it for 15 minutes with the lid on.

Place the hot rice in a shallow bowl, add the sushi vinegar and mix well. Spread the rice thinly on a tray and let it cool to lukewarm.

SESAME SEED SALMON SUSHI

By blending the sesame seeds, your body can access all the good nutrition inside them. For a step-by-step guide to how to roll sushi, see page 21.

Serves 2–3

— **30g white sesame seeds**
— **30g black sesame seeds**
— **300g White sushi rice, cooked and seasoned with sushi vinegar, lukewarm** (see left)
— **1 tsp sesame oil**
— **pinch of sea salt**
— **150g sushi-grade salmon fillet, finely sliced**
— **2 half sheets of dried nori seaweed**
— **1 cucumber, julienne cut**

Mix 20g of both types of sesame seeds in a bowl. Put the remainder in a blender and blitz into a powder. Add this sesame powder to the cooked rice and mix well. Then add the whole sesame seeds to the rice and stir them in, too.

Massage the sesame oil and sea salt on to the salmon and leave for five minutes.

Take about 150g of the rice mix and spread it all over the rough side of a half sheet of nori on a rolling mat.

Flip the sheet upside down so the seaweed is on the top, facing you. It should still be on the mat.

Place half the marinated salmon and cucumber in a row across the seaweed.

Roll, leaving the white rice on the outside. Repeat with the other half nori sheet, rice and filling.

Cut each roll into six pieces, then serve.

SUSHI CUP CAKES

Image on page 108

This is a cute idea and everyone loves them.

Makes 10

— **30g sushi-grade or smoked salmon, finely sliced** (at least 10 pieces)
— **30g sushi-grade sea bream, finely sliced** (at least 10 pieces)
— **30g sushi-grade tuna steak, finely sliced** (at least 10 pieces)
— **2 slices of prosciutto, finely sliced lengthways** (at least 10 pieces)
— **400g White sushi rice, cooked and seasoned with sushi vinegar** (see page 110), **lukewarm**
— **3cm block of cheese, finely cubed**
— **2 oba leaves, or coriander leaves, finely chopped**
— **10g white sesame seeds**

Cut out 10 x 15cm squares of cling film. Place a cling film square on your hand. Put one slice each of salmon, sea bream, tuna and prosciutto in the middle of the cling film.

Put 40g of rice on top of the fish and prosciutto. Close your hand and twist the cling film edges to make a ball. Repeat to make 10 balls. Unwrap from the cling film.

Place each of the balls in a paper cupcake case. Sprinkle with the cheese, oba leaves and sesame seeds to decorate.

BOUQUET OF FLOWERS TEMAKI

Image on page 109

The idea of this is that the filling ingredients should spill out of the top of the sushi cones.

Serves 3–4

— **7 half sheets of dried nori seaweed**
— **420g White sushi rice, cooked and seasoned with sushi vinegar, lukewarm** (see page 110)
— **7 oba leaves**
— **handful of salad leaves**
— **100g sushi-grade or smoked salmon, finely sliced**
— **100g sushi-grade tuna, finely sliced**
— **100g sushi-grade sea bream, finely sliced**
— **½ cucumber, finely sliced**
— **1 avocado, finely sliced**
— **7 cooked prawns, peeled**

Cut seven sheets of greaseproof paper the same size as the sheets of nori.

Place one of the greaseproof paper sheets on your hand and place one half sheet of nori on top, rough side facing you.

Place 60g of rice on to the left-hand side of the sheet of nori, spreading it evenly.

Add one-seventh of the other ingredients across the rice, in a line from top right to bottom left.

Use your thumb to push the bottom corner of nori across to the middle. Then fold the rest of the seaweed around to form in a cone shape.

Repeat to make seven of these rolls. Place in a shallow bowl or vase to look like bouquets.

SALMON, ROE AND AVOCADO SUSHI CAKE

If you are at all nervous of rolling sheets of dried seaweed, this is the recipe for you. It's a doddle. Obviously just scale the recipe up to make more 'cakes'. You will need a metal circle-shaped cutter 8cm wide and 7cm high.

Makes 1 portion

— 80g White sushi rice, cooked and seasoned with sushi vinegar, lukewarm (see page 110)
— 1 avocado, skinned and cut into 1cm pieces
— 50g sushi-grade or smoked salmon, chopped into small pieces
— 25g salmon roe

Place the cutter on to a serving plate. Press 40g of the cooked rice evenly in a layer in the cutter.

Top with an even layer of avocado chunks, then the salmon pieces.

Press in a second layer of rice. Add the roe on top, nice and evenly, then gently pull the cutter away.

FLOWER CAKE

This is an impressive and beautiful thing, sure to wow your guests. To construct it, use a 12cm tart ring. If you line it with cling film, you will find it easier to remove the cake without trouble.

Serves 3–4

For the egg ribbons
— 1 tbsp mirin or caster sugar
— ½ tsp sea salt
— 3 eggs, lightly beaten

For the cake
— 360g White sushi rice, cooked and seasoned with sushi vinegar, lukewarm (see page 110)
— 20g white sesame seeds
— 1 avocado, finely sliced
— 100g sushi-grade tuna steak, cut into 1cm cubes
— 10cm chunk of cucumber, finely sliced into discs
— 50g sushi-grade salmon steak, cut into 1cm cubes
— 150g salmon roe
— beansprouts, or sprigs of coriander, to serve

Start with the egg ribbons. Add the mirin or sugar and salt to the egg. Cook it in a shallow sauté pan to make a thin omelette. When it has cooled down, roll it into a tube and slice it finely into shreds.

Now for the cake. Use a springform tin or a 12cm tart ring lined with cling film. Mix the cooked rice with the white sesame seeds and use this mixture to line the bottom of the tin.

Gently lay the egg ribbons along the outer edge of the rice. Make a concentric circle, next to the egg but within it, of the avocado slices.

Layer cubes of tuna in a circle next to the avocado. Then make a circle of cucumber discs next to the tuna. As you work inwards, place the salmon chunks towards the centre. In the very centre place your salmon roe.

Garnish with beansprouts or sprigs of coriander and serve immediately.

EGG AND EEL SUSHI ROLL

There are strong flavours here, but the rich, oily eel is so very good for you and so utterly delicious. For a step-by-step guide to how to roll sushi, see page 21.

Serves 2–3

— 5 shiitake mushrooms, stems removed, finely sliced
— sea salt
— 1 full sheet of dried nori seaweed
— 300g White sushi rice, cooked and seasoned with sushi vinegar, lukewarm (see page 110)
— 3 x 10cm lengths of cucumber, finely sliced into discs
— 200g packet of roasted eel, sliced into 2cm pieces
— handful of baby spinach, washed
— ½ tsp cornflour
— 1 tsp dashi flakes
— 3 eggs, lightly beaten

Preheat the grill. Grill the mushrooms, sprinkled with sea salt, on both sides, until cooked.

Place the nori sheet, rough side up, on to a sushi rolling mat. Spread the rice evenly all over the nori.

Flip the sheet upside down so the seaweed is on the top, facing you.

Place the cucumber lengths up the nori from the bottom, leaving the top one-third of the nori clear.

Place the roasted eel across the middle of the cucumber. Lay shiitake mushroom slices over the eel, then the spinach over the mushrooms. Put a sushi rolling mat over everything and press it gently to ensure it is held together well.

Add the cornflour, dashi flakes and a pinch more sea salt to the beaten eggs. Make a thin omelette with this in a sauté pan; it should be about 1.5 times bigger than the nori sheet.

Place the egg on to a rolling mat. Place your sushi roll on top. Roll the omelette up with the sushi roll. Leave it whole for a short while, to settle, then cut into six pieces to serve.

FIVE SENSES SUPER-TASTY SALMON SUSHI

As usual, simply scale up the amounts here to feed more people. You can use either tobanjan or the Korean spicy paste gochujang, both can be bought from Asian food stores or online. For a step-by-step guide to how to roll sushi, see page 21.

Serves 1

— 100g sushi-grade salmon
— 1 half sheet of dried nori seaweed
— 150g White sushi rice, cooked and seasoned with sushi vinegar, lukewarm (see page 110)
— 10cm cucumber, finely sliced
— ½ avocado, finely sliced
— 1 spring onion, finely chopped

For the marinade
— 1 tbsp sesame oil
— 1 tsp tobanjan or gochujang
— 1 tbsp sake
— pinch of sea salt

Grill the salmon lightly just so the surface is seared, about one minute on each side, then slice very finely.

Mix together all the ingredients for the marinade and use to coat the salmon slices in a small bowl. Leave to marinate for five minutes.

Place the nori, rough side up, on to a sushi rolling mat. Spread the rice evenly all over.

Flip the sheet upside down so the seaweed is on the top, facing you. It should still be on the mat. Add the cucumber and avocado across the middle of the sheet. Roll it all the way up.

Wrap the salmon around the rice rolls. Put the sushi rolling mat on top of the salmon and squeeze the roll gently to ensure it is held together well. Cut into six or eight pieces.

Sprinkle with the spring onion and serve.

WASABI CREAM CHEESE SUSHI

Red meat and cream cheese aren't ingredients you would usually find in sushi; this is a good way to introduce sushi to more nervous western palates. Scale the recipe up to make more. For a step-by-step guide to how to roll sushi, see page 21.

Serves 1

— **30g lamb steak, finely sliced**
— **150g White sushi rice, cooked and seasoned with sushi vinegar, lukewarm** (see page 110)
— **1 half sheet of dried nori seaweed**
— **10g white and black sesame seeds**
— **30g cream cheese**
— **1 tbsp wasabi**
— **pinch of freshly ground black pepper**
— **7 chives**
— **small handful of rocket salad leaves**

Grill the slices of lamb for five minutes, turning once.

Spread the sushi rice on to the rough side of the nori, on a rolling mat. Sprinkle the sesame seeds evenly on top of the rice.

Flip the sheet upside down so the seaweed is on the top, facing you. It should still be on the mat. Mix the cream cheese with the wasabi and black pepper, then spread it across the middle of the seaweed.

Place the chives, lamb and rocket on top of the cream cheese and roll.

Cut each roll into six pieces, then serve.

DOLL CAKES

Go on, just try to resist these. They are amazingly cute and appeal to the palates of children.

Makes 2 dolls

— **2 quail's eggs**
— **2 regular hen's eggs, lightly beaten**
— **300g White sushi rice, cooked and seasoned with sushi vinegar, lukewarm** (see page 110)
— **1 full sheet of dried nori seaweed**
— **4 sesame seeds** (for eyes)

Hard-boil the quail's eggs in boiling water for 2½–3 minutes, then drain. Peel them carefully. They need to stay as unblemished as possible, as these are the dolls' heads.

Heat a 25cm frying pan and cook the beaten eggs to make a thin omelette.

Mould two cones with the rice. Cut the omelette in two to make two half moon shapes. Wrap each half around the rice cone to create a cloak/kimono.

Cut two strips of nori 1cm thick and 20cm long and wrap one around each cloak/kimono like a belt. Seal with water. Using a toothpick, join a quail's egg to the top of each rice cone body.

Gently push two sesame seeds into each egg to form eyes. Use tiny strips of nori to create hair shapes on top of each egg.

Depending how artistic you are feeling, you can add extra adornments!

PEPPER NIGIRI SUSHI

Nigiri sushi is made by moulding with your hands. For a step-by-step guide to forming it, see page 21.

Makes 12

— **2 peppers** (1 red, 1 yellow)
— **240g White sushi rice, cooked and seasoned with sushi vinegar, lukewarm** (see page 110)
— **sheet of dried nori seaweed**

Grill the peppers, turning, until the skin is blackened on all sides. Leave until cool, then peel the peppers, remove the ribs, stem and seeds and cut each into six neat strips, 6 x 3cm.

Using 20g of rice each time and following my guide (see page 21), make 12 nigiri rice shapes. Place a piece of red or yellow pepper on top of each nigiri.

Cut the nori into 12 x 1cm strips. Wrap the strips of nori around the outer edge of each nigiri to support the pepper.

ZEN SUSHI

I call this 'Zen' because it is vegan, in the tradition of the food eaten by Japanese monks. For a step-by-step guide to how to roll sushi, see page 21.

Serves 1

— **6 asparagus spears**
— **sea salt**
— **4 oyster mushrooms, sliced**
— **20g white sesame seeds**
— **150g White sushi rice, cooked and seasoned with sushi vinegar, lukewarm** (see page 110)
— **half sheet of nori seaweed.**

Steam the asparagus spears over salty water for three or four minutes, or until just becoming tender. Drain very well.

Preheat the grill on its highest setting. Grill the asparagus and mushrooms, sprinkled with sea salt, on both sides, until cooked.

Mix the sesame seeds into the rice.

Place the sheet of nori on a sushi rolling mat, rough side up. Place the rice over the entire sheet of nori. Flip the sheet upside down so the seaweed is on the top, facing you. It should still be on the rolling mat.

Place the asparagus spears and mushrooms across the centre of the seaweed.

Then, using the rolling mat, roll the whole length up. Cut into six pieces, then serve.

SUSHI CANAPÉS

These are easy to make in large batches for a party,
You will need a 3cm cutter. Use the same shape
or different shapes, as you prefer.

Each recipe makes 10

— **200g White sushi rice, cooked
  and seasoned with sushi vinegar,
  lukewarm** (see page 110)

Make 10 bases by packing the cutter with
20g of rice. Add the toppings (see below),
before gently removing the cutter.

CRAB CANAPÉS

— **1 tbsp mayonnaise**
— **pinch of chopped dill, plus spriglets to serve**
— **20g flaked crab**
— **10 parsley leaves, finely chopped**

Mix the mayonnaise and dill together.
Spoon the mayo on to the rice canapé.

Place a small amount of flaked crab
on top and finish with a parsley leaf
and a little dill.

SALMON ROE WASABI CANAPÉS

— **1 tsp wasabi paste**
— **3cm chunk of cucumber, finely chopped**
— **2 tbsp salmon roe**
— **a few pea shoots**

Mix the wasabi and cucumber together.
Spoon this on to the rice canapé.

Place the salmon roe on top of this and
finish with the pea shoots.

FRUITY SALMON FLOWER CANAPÉS

— **10 small slices of melon**
— **5 oba leaves**
— **2 slices of smoked salmon, each cut into 5**

Place a slice of melon on top of the rice canapé.
Cut each oba leaf into 4 and add 2 on top of each
slice of melon (so it looks as if it is the leaf
of a flower).

Roll a smoked salmon piece up to make a flower bud
shape and place it on top.

SPICY COURGETTE CANAPÉS

— **20g white turnip, cut into 5mm cubes**
— **sea salt**
— **3cm length of courgette, sliced into
  5mm strips**
— **10g grated cheddar cheese**
— **1 tsp grapeseed oil**
— **1 tsp wasabi paste**
— **1 tsp maple syrup**

Place the turnip in a bowl, sprinkle with sea
salt and set aside to marinate for 20 minutes.
Drain in a sieve.

Meanwhile, preheat the grill, or heat a griddle
pan. Lightly grill, or griddle, the courgette slices
on both sides for a few minutes. Put a little cheese
on top of each courgette slice and grill for two
minutes. Place a slice of courgette on top of
a rice canapé.

Mix the marinated turnip, grapeseed oil and
wasabi. Spoon this on top of the courgette.

Add a tiny drop of syrup to serve.

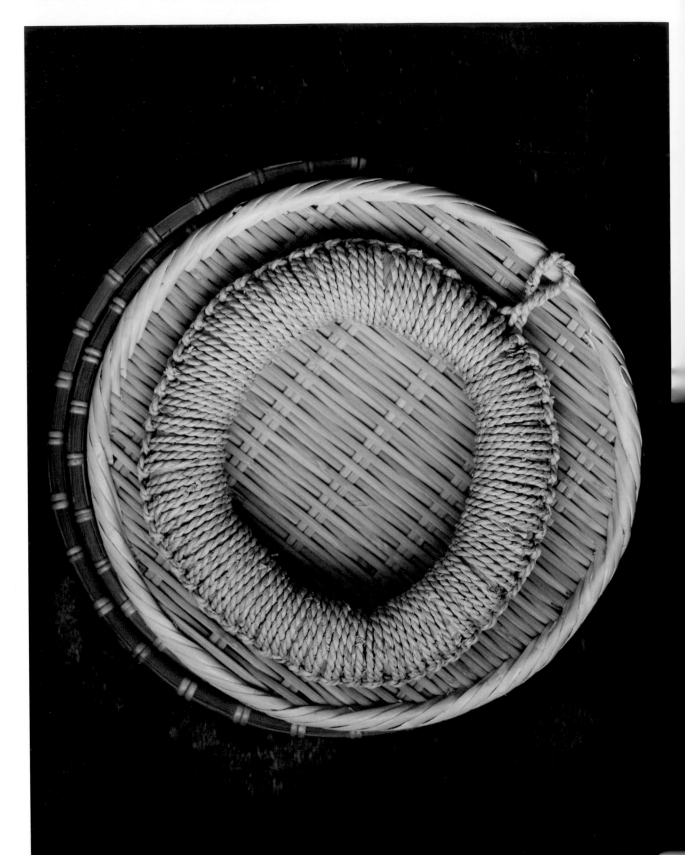

Index

Thanks once again to everyone at Quadrille, especially to Anne Furniss for her continued faith in me and to Helen Lewis for her amazing eye and for finding just the right team to make this such a beautiful book. Lisa Linder, that means you! And to Risa Sano and Aya Nishimura for the design and for making all the food look so incredible.

To Diana Beaumont, for your efficiency, warmth and spot-on judgement. Thank you. To Emma Bannister, for all your experience, patience, hard work and lots of laughs. Thanks to Lucy Bannell, for your work and support.

Most especially, to my mother and my grandmother, Motoko and Teru.

Editorial director Anne Furniss
Creative director Helen Lewis
Project editor Lucy Bannell
Art direction and design Mentsen
Photography Lisa Linder
Editorial consultant Emma Bannister
Food styling Aya Nishimura
Production director Vincent Smith
Production controller Emily Noto

First published in 2015 by Quadrille Publishing Ltd
www.quadrille.co.uk

Text © 2015 Makiko Sano
Photography © 2015 Lisa Linder
Design & layout © 2015 Quadrille Publishing Ltd

British Library Cataloguing-in-Publication Data
A catalogue record for this book is available from the British Library.

ISBN: 978 184949 562 2

Printed in China.

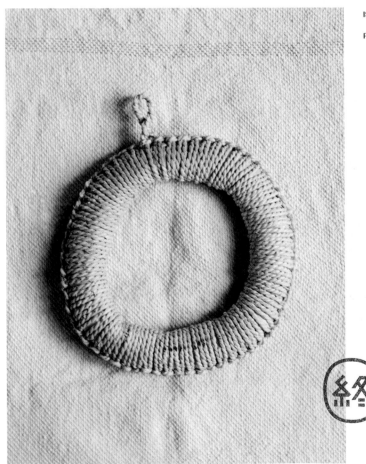